VOLUME III

THE OXFORD
HISTORY OF BRITAIN

This five-volume series, edited by Kenneth O. Morgan, is the work of ten historians who are all distinguished authorities in their fields.

THE OXFORD
HISTORY
OF
BRITAIN

EDITED BY

KENNETH O. MORGAN

VOLUME III

THE TUDORS AND STUARTS

John Guy and John Morrill

Oxford   New York

OXFORD UNIVERSITY PRESS

Oxford University Press, Walton Street, Oxford OX2 6DP

Oxford New York Toronto
Delhi Bombay Calcutta Madras Karachi
Kuala Lumpur Singapore Hong Kong Tokyo
Nairobi Dar es Salaam Cape Town
Melbourne Auckland Madrid

and associated companies in
Berlin Ibadan

Oxford is a trade mark of Oxford University Press

The text of this edition first published 1984
in The Oxford Illustrated History of Britain
Revised text first published by Oxford University Press in five volumes 1992

British Library Cataloguing in Publication Data

Data available

Library of Congress Cataloging in Publication Data
The Oxford history of Britain / edited by Kenneth O. Morgan.
p. cm.
Text based on: The Oxford illustrated history of Britain.
Includes bibliographical references.
Contents: v. 3. The Tudors and Stuarts / John Guy and John Morrill
1. Great Britain—History. I. Morgan, Kenneth O. II. Oxford
illustrated history of Britain.
941—dc20 DA30.093 1992 92-1156
ISBN 0-19-285265-5

3 5 7 9 10 8 6 4

Printed in Great Britain by
Biddles Ltd.
Guildford and King's Lynn

CONTENTS

LIST OF MAPS

1. *The Tudor Age*

(1485–1603)

═══

JOHN GUY

Population Changes

THE age of the Tudors has left its impact on Anglo-American minds as a watershed in British history. Hallowed tradition, native patriotism, and post-imperial gloom have united to swell our appreciation of the period as a true golden age. Names alone evoke a phoenix-glow—Henry VIII, Elizabeth I, and Mary Stuart among the sovereigns of England and Scotland; Wolsey, William Cecil, and Leicester among the politicians; Marlowe, Shakespeare, Hilliard, and Byrd among the creative artists. The splendours of the Court of Henry VIII, the fortitude of Sir Thomas More, the making of the English Bible, Prayer Book, and Anglican Church, the development of Parliament, the defeat of the Armada, the Shakespearian moment, and the legacy of Tudor domestic architecture—these are the undoubted climaxes of a simplified orthodoxy in which genius, romance, and tragedy are superabundant.

Reality is inevitably more complex, less glamorous, and more interesting than myth. The most potent forces within Tudor England were often social, economic, and demographic ones. Thus if the period became a golden age, it was primarily because the considerable growth in population that occurred

between 1500 and the death of Elizabeth I did not so dangerously exceed the capacity of available resources, particularly
food supplies, as to precipitate a Malthusian crisis. Famine and
disease unquestionably disrupted and disturbed the Tudor economy, but they did not raze it to its foundations, as in the
fourteenth century. More positively, the increased manpower
and demand that sprang from rising population stimulated
economic growth and the commercialization of agriculture,
encouraged trade and urban renewal, inspired a housing
revolution, enhanced the sophistication of English manners,
especially in London, and (more arguably) bolstered new
and exciting attitudes among Tudor Englishmen, notably indi-
vidualistic ones derived from Reformation ideals and Calvinist
theology.

The matter is debatable, but there is much to be said for the
view that England was economically healthier, more expansive,
and more optimistic under the Tudors than at any time since
the Roman occupation of Britain. Certainly, the contrast with
the fifteenth century was dramatic. In the hundred or so years
before Henry VII became king of England in 1485, England had
been underpopulated, underdeveloped, and inward-looking
compared with other Western countries, notably France. Her
recovery after the ravages of the Black Death had been slow—
slower than in France, Germany, Switzerland, and some Italian
cities. The process of economic recovery in pre-industrial
societies was basically one of recovery of population, and
figures will be useful. On the eve of the Black Death (1348),
the population of England and Wales was between 4 and 5
millions; by 1377, successive plagues had reduced it to 2.5
millions. Yet the figure for England (without Wales) was still
no higher than 2.26 millions in 1525, and it is transparently
clear that the striking feature of English demographic history
between the Black Death and the reign of Henry VIII is the
stagnancy of population which persisted until the 1520s.
However, the growth of population rapidly accelerated after
1525:

English population totals 1525–1601

Year	Population total in millions
1525	2.26
1541	2.77
1551	3.01
1561	2.98
1581	3.60
1601	4.10

(Source: E. A. Wrigley and R. S. Schofield, *The Population History of England, 1541–1871*, London, 1981)

Between 1525 and 1541 the population of England grew extremely fast, an impressive burst of expansion after long inertia. This rate of growth slackened off somewhat after 1541, but the Tudor population continued to increase steadily and inexorably, with a temporary reversal only in the late 1550s, to reach 4.10 millions in 1601. In addition, the population of Wales grew from about 210,000 in 1500 to 380,000 by 1603.

While England reaped the fruits of the recovery of population in the sixteenth century, however, serious problems of adjustment were encountered. The impact of a sudden crescendo in demand, and pressure on available resources of food and clothing, within a society that was still overwhelmingly agrarian, was to be as painful as it was, ultimately, beneficial. The morale of countless ordinary Englishmen was to be wrecked by problems that were too massive to be ameliorated either by governments or by traditional, ecclesiastical philanthropy. Inflation, speculation in land, enclosures, unemployment, vagrancy, poverty, and urban squalor were the most pernicious evils of Tudor England, and these were the wider symptoms of population growth and agricultural commercialization. In the fifteenth century farm rents had been discounted, because tenants were so elusive; lords had abandoned direct exploitation of their demesnes, which were leased to tenants on favourable terms. Rents had been low, too, on peasants' customary holdings; labour services had been commuted, and servile villeinage had virtually disappeared from the face of the English landscape by 1485. At the same time, money wages had risen to reflect the contraction of the wage-labour force after 1348, and food prices had fallen in reply to reduced market demand. But rising demand after 1500 burst the bubble of artificial prosperity born of stagnant population. Land hunger led to soaring rents. Tenants of farms and copyholders were evicted by business-minded landlords. Several adjacent farms would be conjoined, and amalgamated for profit, by outside investors at the expense of sitting tenants. Marginal land would be converted to pasture for more profitable sheep-rearing. Commons were enclosed, and waste land reclaimed, by landlords or squatters, with consequent extinction of common grazing rights. The literary opinion that the active Tudor land market nurtured a new entrepreneurial class of greedy capitalists grinding the faces of the poor is an exaggeration. Yet it is fair to say that not all landowners, claimants, and squatters were entirely scrupulous in their attitudes; certainly a vigorous market arose among dealers in defective titles to land, with resulting harassment of many legitimate occupiers.

The greatest distress sprang, nevertheless, from inflation and unemployment. High agricultural prices gave farmers strong incentives to produce crops for sale in the dearest markets in nearby towns, rather than for the satisfaction of rural subsistence. Rising population, especially urban population, put intense strain on the markets themselves: demand for food often outstripped supply, notably in years of poor harvests due to epidemics or bad weather. In cash terms, agricultural prices began to rise faster than industrial prices from the beginning of the reign of Henry VIII, a rise which accelerated as the sixteenth century progressed. Yet in real terms, the price rise was even more volatile than it appeared to be, since population growth ensured that labour was plentiful and cheap, and wages low. The size of the work-force in Tudor England increasingly exceeded available employment opportunities; average wages and living standards declined accordingly. Men (and women) were prepared to do a day's work for little more than board wages;

able-bodied persons, many of whom were peasants displaced by rising rents or the enclosure of commons, drifted in waves to the towns in quest of work.

The best price index hitherto constructed covers the period 1264–1954, and its base period is most usefully 1451–75—the end of the fifteenth-century era of stable prices. From this index, we may read the fortunes of the wage-earning consumers of Tudor England, because the calculations are based on the fluctuating costs of composite units of the essential foodstuffs and manufactured goods, such as textiles, that made up an average family shopping basket in southern England at different times. Two indexes are, in fact, available: first the annual price index of the composite basket of consumables; secondly the index of the basket expressed as the equivalent of the annual wage rates of building craftsmen in southern England. No one supposes that building workers were typical of the English labour force in the sixteenth century, or at any other time. But the indexes serve as a rough guide to the appalling reality of the rising household expenses of the majority of Englishmen in the Tudor period.

Indexes (1451–75 = 100) of (1) price of composite unit of consumables; (2) equivalent of wage rate of building craftsman

Year	(1)	(2)
1450	102	98
1490	106	94
1510	103	97
1530	169	59
1550	262	48
1570	300	56
1590	396	51
1610	503	40

(Source: E. H. Phelps Brown and S. V. Hopkins, *Economica*, no. 92, Nov. 1956, n.s. vol. xxiii)

It is clear that in the century after Henry VIII's accession, the average prices of essential consumables rose by some 488 per cent. The price index stood at the 100 or so level until 1513, when it rose to 120. A gradual rise to 169 had occurred by 1530, and a further crescendo to 231 was attained by 1547, the year of Henry VIII's death. In 1555 the index reached 270; two years later, it hit a staggering peak of 409, though this was partly due to the delayed effects of the currency debasements practised by Henry VIII and Edward VI. On the accession of Elizabeth I, in 1558, the index had recovered to a median of 230. It climbed again thereafter, though more steadily: 300 in 1570, 342 in 1580, and 396 in 1590. But the later 1590s witnessed exceptionally meagre harvests, together with regional epidemics and famine: the index read 515 in 1595, 685 in 1598, and only settled back to 459 in 1600.

The index expressed as the equivalent of the building craftsman's wages gives an equally sober impression of the vicissitudes of Tudor domestic life. An abrupt decline in the purchasing power of wages occurred between 1510 and 1530, the commodity equivalent falling by some 40 per cent in twenty years. The index fell again in the 1550s, but recovered in the next decade to a position equivalent to two-thirds of its value in 1510. Apart from 1586–7, it then remained more or less stable until the 1590s, when it collapsed to 39 in 1595, and to 29 in 1597. On the queen's death in 1603 it had recovered to a figure of 45—which meant that real wages had dropped by 57 per cent since 1500.

These various data establish the most fundamental truth about the age of the Tudors. When the percentage change of English population in the sixteenth century is plotted against that of the index of purchasing power of a building craftsman's wages over the same period, it is immediately plain that the two lines of development are opposite and commensurate (see graph). Living standards declined as the population rose; recovery began as population growth abated and collapsed between 1556 and 1560. Standards then steadily dropped again, until previous proportions were overthrown by the disasters of 1586–7 and 1594–8—though the cumulative increase in the size of the wage-labour force since 1570 must also have had distorting effects.

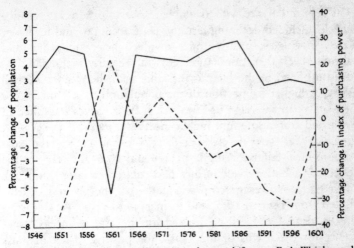

—— Percentage change of population since last total (Source: E. A. Wrigley and R. S. Schofield, *The Population History of England, 1541–1871*, London, 1981)

--- Percentage change since last total (averaged over three years) in index of purchasing power of building craftsman's wages as compared to index of his purchasing power in 1510 (Source: E. H. Phelps Brown and S. V. Hopkins, *Economica*, no. 92, Nov. 1956, n.s. vol. xxiii)

In other words, population trends, rather than government policies, capitalist entrepreneurs, European imports of American silver, the more rapid circulation of money, or even currency debasements, were the key factor in determining the fortunes of the British Isles in the sixteenth century. English government expenditure on warfare, heavy borrowing, and debasements unquestionably exacerbated inflation and unemployment. But the basic facts of Tudor life were linked to population growth.

In view of this fundamental truth, the greatest triumph of Tudor England was its ability to feed itself. A major national subsistence crisis was avoided. Malthus, who wrote his historic *Essay on the Principle of Population* in 1798, listed positive and preventive checks as the traditional means by which population was kept in balance with available resources of food. Preventive checks included declining fertility, contraception, and fewer, or later, marriages; positive ones involved heavy mortality and abrupt reversal of population growth. Fertility in England indeed declined in the later 1550s, and again between 1566 and 1571. A higher proportion of the population than hitherto did not marry in the reign of Elizabeth I. Poor harvests resulted in localized starvation, and higher mortality, in 1481–3, 1519–21, 1527–9, 1544–5, 1549–51, 1554–6, 1586–7, and 1594–7, the most serious crop failures being in 1555–6 and 1596–7. In fact, as the effect of a bad harvest in any particular year lasted until the next good or average crop was gathered, the severest dearths lasted from 1555 to 1557, and from 1596 to 1598. Yet devastating as dearth and disease proved for the affected areas, especially for the towns of the 1590s, the positive check of mass mortality on a national scale was absent even during the influenza epidemic of 1555–9. True, in addition to its other difficulties, Mary's regime faced the most serious mortality crisis since the Black Death: the population of England dropped by 200,000, or by six per cent. But since some regions were relatively lightly affected, it is not proved that this was a national crisis in terms of its geographical extent. Also, population growth was only temporarily interrupted. Indeed, the chronology, intensity, and restricted geographical range of famine in the sixteenth century suggest that starvation crises in England were abating, rather than worsening, over time, while epidemics took fewer victims than before in proportion to the expansion of population. The countryside escaped crisis during two-thirds of Elizabeth's reign and the rural population remained in surplus. When the towns suffered an excess of deaths over births, this surplus was sufficient both to increase the numbers who stayed on the land and to compensate for urban losses by migration to towns.

So there is much to be said for an optimistic view of the age of the Tudors. The sixteenth century saw the birth of Britain's pre-industrial political economy—an evolving accommodation between population and resources, economics and politics, ambition and rationality. England abandoned the disaster-oriented framework of the Middle Ages for the new dawn of low-pressure equilibrium. Progress had its price, unalterably paid by the weak, invariably banked by the strong. Yet the tyranny of the price index was not ubiquitous. Wage rates for agricultural workers fell by less than for building workers, and some privileged groups of wage-earners such as the Mendip miners may have enjoyed a small rise in real income. Land-owners, commercialized farmers, and property investors were the most obvious beneficiaries of a system that guaranteed fixed expenses and enhanced selling prices—it was in the Tudor period that the nobility, gentry, and mercantile classes alike came to appreciate fully the enduring qualities of land. But many wage-labouring families were not wholly dependent upon their wages for subsistence. Multiple occupations, domestic self-employment, and cottage industries flourished, especially in the countryside; town-dwellers grew vegetables, kept animals, and brewed beer, except in the confines of London. Wage-labourers employed by great households received meat and drink in addition to cash income, although this customary practice was on the wane by the 1590s.

Finally, it is not established that vagabondage or urban population outside London expanded at a rate faster than the general rate of increase in national population. It used to be argued that the English urban population climbed from 6.2 per cent of the national total in 1520 to 8.4 per cent by the end of the century. However, London's spectacular growth alone ex-plains this apparent over-population: the leading provincial towns, Norwich, Bristol, Coventry, and York, grew slightly or remained stable in absolute terms—and must thus have been inhabited by a reduced share of population in proportional terms.

Henry VII

Yet if the new dawn was marked by low-pressure equilib-rium, the quest for political stability at the end of the fifteenth century remained of paramount importance to future progress. No one now thinks that the thirty years' internal commotion known as the Wars of the Roses amounted to more than an intermittent interruption of national life, or that Henry VII's victory at Bosworth Field (22 August 1485) rates credit beyond that due to luck and good fortune. Bosworth Field was, indeed, conclusive only because Richard III, together with so many of his household men and supporters, was slain in the battle; because Richard had eliminated in advance the most plausible alternatives to Henry VII; and because Henry was ingenious enough to proclaim himself king with effect from the day before the battle, thus enabling the Ricardian rump to be deemed traitors. By marrying Elizabeth of York, daughter of Edward IV, Henry VII then proffered the essential palliative to those Yorkist defectors who had joined him against Richard in the first place—the ensuing births of Arthur in 1486, Margaret in 1489, Henry in 1491, and Mary in 1496 achieved the 'Union of the Two Noble and Illustrious Families of Lancaster and York' upon which the pro-Tudor chronicler Edward Hall lavished the praise echoed by Shakespeare.

But the need for stability went far beyond Henry VII's accession and marriage. The victor of Bosworth Field could found a new dynasty; it remained to be seen whether he could create a new monarchy. The essential demand was that someone should restore the English Crown to its former position above mere aristocratic faction. The king should not simply reign; he should also rule. For too long, the king of England had been 'first among equals', rather than 'king and emperor'. The Wars of the Roses had done negligible permanent damage to agriculture, trade, and industry, but they had undermined confidence in monarchy as an institution: the king was seen to be unable, or unwilling, to protect the rights of all his subjects. In particular, royal government had ceased to be politically neutral, having been excessively manipulated by individuals as an instrument of faction. All aspects of the system, especially the legal system, had been deeply permeated by family loyalties, aristocratic rivalries, favouritism, and a web of personal connections.

In fairness to Edward IV, whom Sir Thomas More thought had left his realm 'in quiet and prosperous estate', the work of reconstruction had already been started. Edward IV's failure to make sufficient progress was primarily due to his excessive generosity, his divisive marriage to Elizabeth Woodville, and his barely-controlled debauchery. His premature death had become the cue for the usurpation of Richard III, who was leader of a large and unusually powerful northern faction. Henry VII was, by contrast, dedicated and hard-working, astute and ascetic, and financially prudent to the point of avarice, or even rapacity, as some have maintained. Yet Henry's ace in the campaign for stability was that his good luck in sweeping the board at Bosworth, as in the case of William the Conqueror in 1066, had freed him, temporarily at least, from dependence on any one group or faction. Henry's continued independence and security naturally had to be earned, consolidated, and defended—a formidable task that absorbed many years. In fact, the first of the Tudor kings had specifically to combine the task of restoring the monarchy with that of protecting its flank from hyperactive Yorkist conspiracy.

Of the two Yorkist impostures, that of Lambert Simnel as earl of Warwick in 1487, although the more exotic, was, thanks to Irish support, the more menacing; that of Perkin Warbeck, as Richard of York during the 1490s, was more easily contained despite Scottish involvement. Simnel was routed at Stoke (16 June 1487); his promoters were killed or pardoned, and the young imposter was taken into the royal household as a servant. Warbeck fell into Henry's hands in August 1497; before long he had abused the king's leniency and was hanged in 1499. His demise was then made an occasion for executing the real earl of Warwick. But it was another seven years before the incarceration in the Tower of Edmund de la Pole, duke of Suffolk, completed the defensive process.

By that time, it was clear that Henry VII, if not to be

distinguished as the inventor of new methods of government, had, nevertheless, mastered the art of streamlining the old. The touchstone of his policy was enforcement—the enforcement of political and financial obligation to the Crown, as much as of law and order. In achieving the restoration of the monarchy, the Tudors practised their belief that ability, good service, and loyalty to the regime, irrespective of a man's social origins and background, were to be the primary grounds of appointments, promotions, favours, and rewards. This belief was most evident in Henry VII's use of royal patronage and in his appointments of ministers and councillors. Patronage was the process by which the Crown awarded grants of offices, lands, pensions, annuities, or other valuable perquisites to its executives and dependants, and was thus its principal weapon of political control, its most powerful motor of political management. Subjects, from great peers of the realm to humble knights and gentry, vied with each other for a share of the spoils—no nobleman was too high to join in the undignified scramble. Henry VII gradually restructured the patronage system to reflect more realistically the Crown's limited resources, and next ensured that the values of grants made under the great seal were fully justified in terms of return on expenditure. The resources of Tudor monarchy were relatively meagre in the years before the Dissolution of the Monasteries, and again in the later part of Elizabeth I's reign. Henry VII set the pace and the standards for distributing royal bounty for much of the sixteenth century; indeed, the only danger inherent in the Tudor model of cash efficiency was that it might veer towards meanness or excessive stringency. The level and flow of grants might become so far diminished in relation to expectations as to ferment impatience, low morale, and even active disloyalty among the Crown's servants and suitors.

Henry VII's ministers were all personally selected by the king for their ability, assiduity, shrewdness, and loyalty—again a pattern for the most part emulated by his Tudor successors. Yet at first sight, Reynold Bray, Richard Empson, and Edmund

Dudley seemed to hold quite minor offices. Bray was Chancellor of the duchy of Lancaster; soon after he died, in 1503, Empson succeeded him; Dudley was 'president of the Council', which effectively meant minister without portfolio. But Bray and the rest exercised control, under the king, far in excess of their apparent status. For Henry VII managed in an absurdly short space of time to erect a network of financial and administrative checks and blueprints, the records of which never left the hands of himself and the selected few, and the methods of which were equally of their own devising. Financial accounting, the exploitation of the undervalued resources of the Crown lands along the most modern lines known to the land-holding aristocracy, the collection of fines and obligations, and the enforcement of Henry VII's morally-dubious but probably necessary system of compelling political opponents, or even apparent friends, to enter into coercive bonds for good behaviour—these vital matters were dealt with only by the king and his inner ring. It was a system that owed nothing to Parliament; it owed something to the Council in so far as Bray and the others sat there as Henry's most trusted councillors; but it owed everything to the king himself, whose vigilance and attention to detail were invincible. Nothing slipped past Henry's keen eye, least of all money through his twitching fingers. The extant Chamber books, the master-documents of the early Henrician nexus of administrative co-ordination, are signed, and thus checked, on every page, and even beside every entry, by the king who was the best businessman ever to sit on the English throne.

Tudor government, however, was as much a question of partnership as of dictatorship. England lacked a police force and a standing army. Revenues increasingly failed to match the expanding functions of central bureaucracy and costs of warfare. James Harrington wrote in *Oceana*, first published in 1656, that government could be based either upon a nobility or upon an army. He was right; in the absence of the permanent militia, the Crown ruled in part through its territorial magnates. It was

for Henry VII and his successors at best to subdue, at worst
to preside over, aristocratic faction, while steering the private
resources of the peerage along lines compatible with royal
interests. In short, 'overmighty subjects', whose persistence was
lamented by Sir John Fortescue in the fifteenth century, and
Francis Bacon in the seventeenth, were essential to the running
of the country. For it was less 'overmighty subjects' that led to
disorder than 'undermighty kings'. Both Henry VII and Henry
VIII appreciated this: between them, they tamed the nobility in
order to ride upon its back.

Henry VII's methods here were a judicious combination of
carrot and stick. In his large and active King's Council, the first
of the Tudors practised consultation in a way that inspired,
alternately, participation and boredom. All noblemen might be
councillors before the reform of the Council by Henry VIII
in late 1536, and political identity depended on attending
Council meetings from time to time. At Westminster the Council sat in Star Chamber (literally *camera stellata*, the room's
azure ceiling being decorated with stars of gold leaf), which
was both a meeting place for the working Council and a court
of law. When Parliament was not in session, Star Chamber
formed the chief point of contact between the Crown, its ministers, and the nobility until Wolsey's fall in 1529, and under
Henry VII it discussed those issues, such as internal security,
the armed defences, and foreign affairs, which, of necessity, had
to secure the support of the magnates, who were also the
muster-men and captains of armies. The Council never debated
fiscal or enforcement policies under Henry VII, matters which
remained firmly vested in the hands of ministers and those of
two tribunals known as the Council Learned in the Law and
the Conciliar Court of Audit. But by making conciliar involvement a dimension of magnate status, Henry VII went far towards filtering out the threat of an alienated nobility that
sprang from lack of communications and isolation in the political wilderness.

Next, Henry VII made an overtly determined bid to concentrate the command of castles and garrisons, and, as far as possible, the supervision of military functions, in the members of the royal Household, and he launched direct attacks on the local, territorial powers of the magnates, if he felt that those powers had been exercised in defiance of perceived royal interests. Such attacks normally took one of two forms, either that of prosecutions and fines at law for misfeasance, or the more drastic resort of attainder and forfeiture.

George Neville, Lord Bergavenny, for instance, was tried in King's Bench in 1507 on a charge of illegally retaining what amounted to a private army. He pleaded guilty (people did under Henry VII, for it was cheaper), and was fined £70,650, being the price, at the rate of £5 per man per month, for which he was liable for having hired 471 men for 30 months from 10 June 1504 to 9 December 1506. It seems that the 'army' comprised 25 gentlemen, 4 clerics, 440 yeomen, one cobbler, and one tinker—the Tudors got details right. But Henry VII was not opposing retaining on principle on the occasion of this prosecution; he *valued* Bergavenny's force, down to that last Kentish tinker, just as much as did its true territorial proprietor—it was even better that Bergavenny was footing the bill. Despite Henry VII's peaceful foreign policy, England was within the mainstream of European affairs, quite apart from her fluctuating relations with Scotland. The all-too-brief marriage of Prince Arthur to Catherine of Aragon in 1501 considerably raised Henry VII's stature in Europe, while his treaty with Anne of Brittany obliged him briefly to invade France in 1492. England, or rather the king of England, had virtually no army beyond that recruited on demand from the royal demesne, and that provided on request by the nobility. Thus, in Bergavenny's case, which was exemplary and admonitory, it was especially relevant that the accused was by birth a Yorkist, and that he had been implicated in an unsuccessful rising of Cornishmen in 1497.

Yet far more drastic, and effective, was the weapon of attainder and forfeiture. Acts of attainder were parliamentary statutes proclaiming convictions for treason, and declaring the victim's property forfeit to the king and his blood 'corrupted'. The method almost always involved execution of the victim, but did not necessarily lead to the total forfeiture of his lands. Most attainders were by tradition repealed later in favour of the heirs, though not always with full restoration of property. Henry VII's reign saw 138 persons attainted, and 86 of these attainders were never reversed. Only 46 were reversed by Henry VII, and six by Henry VIII. These figures compare unfavourably with those of the reigns of Henry VI, Edward IV, and even Richard III— reflecting the toughness of Tudor policy. Henry VII realized that attainders were not simply a tool of faction and dynastic intrigue: they could be used to excise 'overmighty' or hostile magnates, while at the same time significantly augmenting the Crown's own power and income. In similar fashion, Henry VIII, after the Pilgrimage of Grace (1536), and Elizabeth I, after the Northern Rising (1569), used attainders to bolster the Crown's territorial strength and eradicate magnate resistance. Finesse was, however, required if the method was not to back-fire. Its excessive use, and repeated failure to reverse attainders in favour of heirs, could spark resentment among the peerage, whose partnership with the monarchy was thus impaired. Attainders could also do serious damage if they left a power vacuum in a particular local area, as occurred in East Anglia when the third duke of Norfolk was attainted by Henry VIII in 1547. His attainder, reversed by Mary in 1553, created instability which the Crown could not easily correct, and paved the way for Ket's Rebellion in 1549.

Historians suspect that Henry VII overdid his policy of enforcement in the latter part of his reign. In 1506, he commissioned one Polydore Vergil, who was a visiting collector of papal taxes, to write a history of England, and it was Polydore who opined that the first of the Tudors had practised financial rapacity after 1502.

For he began to treat his people with more harshness and severity than had been his custom, in order (as he himself asserted) to ensure that they remained more thoroughly and entirely in obedience to him. The people themselves had another explanation for his action, for they considered they were suffering not on account of their own sins but on account of the greed of their monarch. It is not indeed clear whether at the start it was greed; but afterwards greed did become apparent.

The debate concerning Henry's rapacity still rages. Whatever the eventual outcome, three points are proven. First, Henry VII used penal bonds in sums ranging from £100 to £10,000 to enforce what *he* considered to be acceptable behaviour on his subjects. These bonds aimed to hold the political nation, especially the nobility, at the king's mercy, and to short-circuit due process of common law in case of offence by the victims. If a man was deemed to have misbehaved, he would simply be sued for debt on his bond—it was not possible to litigate over the nature or extent of the alleged offence. In other words, Henry VII used bonds to defeat the law in the way that King John and Richard II had used blank charters. Second, Empson and Dudley corrupted juries to find verdicts in favour of Henry VII's feudal rights. The best example is the case of the estates of the earl of Westmorland. A conciliar inquiry had to be launched to rectify this matter in Henry VIII's reign. Lastly, Henry VII sold offices, including legal ones. He twice sold the chief justiceship of the Court of Common Pleas, and at high prices. He also sold the posts of Attorney-General, Master of the Rolls, and Speaker of the House of Commons.

Henry VIII

Henry VIII's accession in 1509 was greeted with feasting, dancing, and rejoicing. He succeeded at barely eighteen years of age, because his elder brother, Arthur, had died in 1502. Under pressure from his councillors, essentially his father's executors, Henry began his 'triumphant' reign by marrying his late brother's widow, Catherine of Aragon—a union that was to have momentous, not to say revolutionary, consequences. He continued by executing Empson and Dudley, who were thrown to the wolves to win popularity. The trick worked—no one complained that the Council omitted to cancel the last batches of outstanding bonds until well into the 1520s. Yet Henry VIII had started as he meant to go on; a glimpse of his vindictiveness was revealed.

Henry VIII's character was certainly fascinating, threatening, and sometimes morbid. His egoism, self-righteousness, and capacity to brood sprang from the fusion of an able but second-rate mind with what looks suspiciously like an inferiority complex. Henry VII had restored stability and royal authority, but it may have been for reasons of character, as much as policy, that his son resolved to augment his regal power. As his reign unfolded Henry VIII added 'imperial' concepts of kingship to existing 'feudal' ones; he sought to give the words 'king and emperor' a meaning unseen since the days of the Roman empire. He was eager, too, to conquer—to emulate the glorious victories of the Black Prince and Henry V, to quest after the golden fleece that was the French Crown. He wished, in fact, to revive the Hundred Years War, despite the success of Valois France in consolidating its territory and the shift of emphasis of European politics towards Italy and Spain. Repeatedly the efforts of his more constructive councillors were bedevilled, and overthrown, by his chivalric dreams, and by costly wars that wasted men, money, and equipment. If, however, humanist criticism of warfare by Colet, Erasmus, and Thomas More is well known, it should not be forgotten that 'honour' in the Renaissance was necessarily defended in the last resort by battle. 'Honour' was the cornerstone of aristocratic culture; sovereign rulers argued that unlike their subjects they lacked 'superiors' from whom redress of grievances might be sought, and so had no choice but to accept the 'arbitrament' of war when diplomacy failed. Also war was the 'sport of kings'. By competing dynastically and territorially with his European counterparts, especially Francis I, Henry VIII acknowledged settled convention and, even more obviously, popular demand. His reign saw the boldest and most extensive invasions of France since the reign of Henry V. In fact, only a minority of contemporaries had any sense of the serious long-term economic damage that Renaissance warfare could inflict.

Evaluation is always a matter of emphasis, but on the twin issues of monarchic theory and lust for conquest, there is everything to be said for the view that Henry VIII's policy was consistent throughout his reign; that Henry was himself directing that policy; and that his ministers and officials were allowed freedom of action only within accepted limits, and when the king was too busy to take a personal interest in state affairs.

Cardinal Wolsey was Henry VIII's first minister, and the fourteen years of that proud but efficient prelate's ascendancy (1515–29) saw the king in a comparatively restrained mood. Henry, unlike his father, found writing 'both tedious and painful'; he preferred hunting, dancing, dallying, and playing the lute. In his more civilized moments, Henry studied theology and astronomy; he would wake up Sir Thomas More in the middle of the night in order that they might gaze at the stars from the roof of a royal palace. He wrote songs, and the words of one form an epitome of Henry's youthful sentiments.

> Pastime with good company
> I love and shall until I die.
> Grudge who lust, but none deny;
> So God be pleased, thus live will I;
>> For my pastance,
>> Hunt, sing and dance;
>> My heart is set
>> All goodly sport
>> For my comfort:
>> Who shall me let?

Yet Henry himself set the tempo; his pastimes were only pursued while he was satisfied with Wolsey. Appointed Lord Chancellor and Chief Councillor on Christmas eve 1515, Wolsey used the Council and Star Chamber as instruments of ministerial power in much the way that Henry VII had used them as vehicles of royal power—though Wolsey happily pursued uniform and equitable ideals of justice in Star Chamber in place of Henry VII's selective justice linked to fiscal advantage. But Wolsey's greatest asset was the unique position he obtained with regard to the English Church. Between them, Henry and Wolsey bludgeoned the pope into granting Wolsey the rank of legate *a latere* for life, which meant that he became the superior ecclesiastical authority in England, and could convoke legatine synods. Using these powers, Wolsey contrived to subject the entire English Church and clergy to a massive dose of Tudor government and taxation, and it looks as if an uneasy compromise prevailed behind the scenes in which Henry agreed that the English Church was, for the moment, best controlled by a churchman who was a royal servant, and the clergy accepted that it was better to be obedient to an ecclesiastical rather than a secular tyrant—for it is unquestionably true that Wolsey protected the Church from the worst excesses of lay opinion while in office.

The trouble was that, with stability restored, and the Tudor dynasty apparently secure, England had started to become vulnerable to a mounting release of forces. It used to be argued that anti-clericalism was a major cause of the English Reformation, but this interpretation has lately been challenged. Recent research has established that the majority of late medieval English clergy were not negligent or unqualified: Church courts were not usually unfair; probate, mortuary, and tithes disputes were few; pluralism, absenteeism, nepotism, sexual misconduct, and commercial 'moonlighting' by clergy were less serious than once was thought. On the other hand, there *were* priests who failed to hold services at the proper times, who did not preach, and whose habits were aggressive—the rector of Addington in Northamptonshire, cited before the Lincoln consistory court in 1526, had two children by his cook and marched about the village in chain-mail. In fact, it was all too easy for a priest to behave like other villagers: to make a mistress of his housekeeper, and to spend the day cultivating his glebe. Although the English Church was free of major scandals, such abuses as non-residence, pluralism, concubinage, and the parochial clergy's neglect to repair chancels, where these occurred, continued to attract attention. Also tithes disputes, probate and mortuary fees, charges for saying mass on special occasions, and the trial and burning of heretics could become flash-points. In particular, it was pointed out by prominent writers, notably the grave and learned Christopher St. German (1460–1541), that the Church's procedure in cases of suspected heresy permitted secret accusations, hearsay evidence, and denied accused persons the benefit of purgation by oath-helpers or trial by jury, which was a Roman procedure contrary to the principles of native English common law—a clerical plot to deprive Englishmen of their natural, legal rights. Such ideas were manifestly explosive; for they incited intellectual affray between clergy and common lawyers.

Late medieval religion was also sacramental and institutional: it could appear to be dominated by 'objective' ritual and ceremony at the expense of 'subjective' religious experience based on Bible reading at home. As the expectations of the educated laity mirrored those of the Renaissance, many people sought to found their faith on texts of Scripture and Bible stories (preferably illustrated ones), but vernacular Bibles were illegal in England—the Church authorities believed that the availability of an English Bible, even an authorized version, would ferment heresy by permitting Englishmen to form their own opinions. Sir Thomas More, Wolsey's successor as Lord Chancellor, declared in his proclamation of 22 June 1530 that 'it is not necessary the said Scripture to be in the English tongue and in the hands of the common people, but that the distribution of the said Scripture, and the permitting or denying thereof, dependeth only upon the discretion of the superiors, as they shall think it convenient'. More pursued a policy of strict censorship: no books in English printed outside the realm on *any* subject whatsoever were to be imported; he forbade the printing of Scriptural or religious books in England, too, unless approved in advance by a bishop. But More and the bishops were swimming against the tide. The invention of printing had revolutionized the transmission of new ideas across Western Europe, including Protestant ideas. Heretical books and Bibles poured from the presses of English exiles abroad, notably that of William Tyndale at Antwerp. The demand for vernacular Scriptures was persistent, insistent, and widespread; Henry VIII was enlightened enough to wish to assent to it, and publication of an official English Bible in Miles Coverdale's translation was first achieved in 1535, the year of More's death.

Of the forces springing from the European Renaissance, Christian Humanism and the influence of Greek learning came first. The humanists, of whom the greatest was Erasmus of Rotterdam (1467–1536), rejected scholasticism in favour of simple biblical piety, or *philosophia Christi*, which was founded on primary textual scholarship, and in particular study of the Greek New Testament. Erasmus made several visits to England, and it was in Cambridge in 1511–14 that he worked upon the Greek text of his edition of the New Testament.

But the renaissance of Greek learning owed as much to a native Englishman, John Colet, the gloomy dean of St. Paul's and founder of its school. Colet, who was also young Thomas More's spiritual director, had been to Italy, where he had encountered the neoplatonist philosophy of Marsilio Ficino and Pico della Mirandola. He had mastered Greek grammar and literature, which he then helped to foster at Oxford and at his school, and the fruits of his philosophical and literary knowledge were applied to Bible study—especially to the works of St. Paul. The result was a method of Scriptural exegesis that broke new ground. Colet emphasized the unity of divine truth, a literal approach to texts, concern for historical context, and belief in a personal and redemptive Christ. These exciting ideas inspired both Erasmus and the younger generation of humanists.

The humanists first challenged the English establishment in 1512 when, preaching before Convocation, Colet attacked clerical abuses and demanded reform of the Church from within.

His sermon caused resentment but the humanists continued to call for spiritual renewal. Erasmus embellished his evangelism with racy criticisms of priests and monks, Catholic superstition, and even the papacy. He published his *Handbook of a Christian Knight* (1503), *Praise of Folly* (1511), and *Education of a Christian Prince* (1516) before Luther challenged the papacy. Also in 1516 he published his Greek New Testament together with a revised Latin translation. Scholars and educated laymen were delighted; at last they drank the pure waters of the fountain-head.

More's *Utopia* (1516) was more complex. It wittily idealized an imaginary society of pagans living on a remote island in accordance with principles of natural virtue. The Utopians possessed reason but lacked Christian revelation, and by implicitly comparing their benign social customs and enlightened attitudes with the inferior standards, in practice, of Christian Europeans, More produced an indictment of the latter based largely on deafening silence. For the irony and scandal was that Christians had so much to learn from heathens.

Yet the humanism of Erasmus and More was fragile. Even without Luther's challenge it would have become fragmented because faith and reason in its scheme were at odds. More's solution was to argue that faith was the superior power and that Catholic beliefs must be defended because God commanded them, but Erasmus trusted human rationality and could not accept that God tested people's faith by making them believe things that Renaissance scholarship had thrown into question. Even Luther regarded Erasmus as an enemy because of his emphasis on reason. So these fissures weakened humanism and new exponents of reform caught public attention. In England, the influence of Lutheranism exceeded the small number of converts: the rise of the 'new learning', as it was called, became the most potent of the forces released in the 1520s and 1530s. Luther's ideas and numerous books rapidly penetrated the universities, especially Cambridge, the City of London, the inns of court, and even reached Henry VIII's Household through the intervention of Anne Boleyn and her circle. At Cambridge, the young scholars influenced included Thomas Cranmer and Matthew Parker, both of whom later became Archbishops of Canterbury. Wolsey naturally made resolute efforts as legate to stamp out the spread of Protestantism, but without obvious success. His critics blamed his reluctance to burn men for heresy—for Wolsey would burn books and imprison men, but shared the humane horror of Erasmus at the thought of himself committing bodies to the flames. However, the true reason for Luther's appeal was that he had given coherent doctrinal expression to the religious subjectivity of individuals, and to their distrust of Rome and papal monarchy. In addition his view of the ministry mirrored the instincts of the laity, and his answer to concubinage was the global solution of clerical marriage.

Into this religious maelstrom dropped Henry VIII's first divorce. Although Catherine of Aragon had borne five children, only the Princess Mary (b. 1516) had survived, and the king demanded the security of a male heir to protect the fortunes of the Tudor dynasty. It was clear by 1527 that Catherine was past the age of childbearing; meanwhile Henry coveted Anne Boleyn, who would not comply without the assurance of marriage. Yet royal annulments were not infrequent, and all might have been resolved without drama, or even unremarked, had not Henry VIII been a proficient, if mendacious, theologian.

The chief obstacle was that Henry, who feared international humiliation, insisted that his divorce should be granted by a competent authority in England—this way he could deprive his wife of her legal rights, and bully his episcopal judges. But his marriage had been founded on Pope Julius II's dispensation, necessarily obtained by Henry VII to enable the young Henry VIII to marry his brother's widow in the first place, and hence the matter pertained to Rome. In order to have his case decided without reference to Rome, in face of the papacy's unwillingness to concede the matter, Henry had to prove against the reigning pope, Clement VII, that his predecessor's dispensation was invalid—then the marriage would automatically terminate, on the grounds that it had never legally existed. Henry would be a bachelor again. However, this strategy took the king away from matrimonial law into the quite remote and hypersensitive realm of papal power. If Julius II's dispensation was invalid, it must be because the successors of St. Peter had no power to devise such instruments, and the popes were thus no better than other human legislators who had exceeded their authority.

Henry was a good enough theologian to know that there *was* a minority opinion in Western Christendom to precisely this effect. He was enough of an egoist, too, to fall captive to his own powers of persuasion—soon he believed that papal primacy was unquestionably a sham, a ploy of human invention to deprive kings and emperors of their legitimate inheritances. Henry looked back to the golden days of the British imperial past, to the time of the Emperor Constantine and of King Lucius I. In fact, Lucius I had never existed—he was a myth, a figment of pre-Conquest imagination. But Henry's British 'sources' showed that this Lucius was a great ruler, the first Christian king of Britain, who had endowed the British Church with all its liberties and possessions, and then written to Pope Eleutherius asking him to transmit the Roman laws. However, the pope's reply explained that Lucius did not need any Roman law, because he already had the *lex Britanniae* (whatever that was) under which he ruled both Church and State:

For you be God's vicar in your kingdom, as the psalmist says, 'Give the king thy judgments, O God, and thy righteousness to the king's son' (Ps. lxxii: 1) . . . A King hath his name of ruling, and not of having a realm. You shall be a king, while you rule well; but if you do otherwise, the name of a king shall not remain with you . . . God grant you so to rule the realm of Britain, that you may reign with him for ever, whose vicar you be in the realm.

Vicarius Dei—vicar of Christ. Henry's divorce had led him, incredibly, to believe in his royal supremacy over the English Church.

With the advent of the divorce crisis, Henry took personal charge of his policy and government. He ousted Wolsey, who was hopelessly compromised in the new scheme of things, since his legatine power came directly from Rome. He named Sir Thomas More to the chancellorship, but this move backfired owing to More's scrupulous reluctance to involve himself in Henry's proceedings. He summoned Parliament, which for the first time in English history worked with the king as an omni-competent legislative assembly, if hesitatingly so. Henry and Parliament finally threw off England's allegiance to Rome in an unsurpassed burst of revolutionary statute-making: the Act of Annates (1532), the Act of Appeals (1533), the Act of Supremacy (1534), the First Act of Succession (1534), the Treasons Act (1534), and the Act against the Pope's Authority (1536). The Act of Appeals proclaimed Henry VIII's new imperial status—all English jurisdiction, both secular and religious, now sprang from the king—and abolished the pope's right to decide English ecclesiastical cases. The Act of Supremacy declared that the king of England was supreme head of the Church of England—not the pope. The Act of Succession was the first of a series of Tudor instruments used to settle the order of succession to the throne, a measure which even Thomas More agreed was in itself sound, save that this statute was prefaced by a preamble denouncing papal jurisdiction as a 'usurpation' of Henry's imperial power. More, together with Bishop Fisher of Rochester, and the London Carthusians, the most ascetic and honourable custodians of papal primacy and the legitimacy of the Aragonese marriage, were tried for 'denying' Henry's supremacy under the terms of the Treasons Act. These terms made it high treason maliciously to deprive either king or queen of 'the dignity, title, or name of their royal estates'—that is to deny Henry's royal supremacy. The victims of the act, who were in reality martyrs to Henry's vindictiveness, were cruelly executed in the summer of 1535. A year later the Reformation legislation was completed by the Act against the Pope's Authority, which removed the last vestiges of papal power in England, including the pope's 'pastoral' right as a teacher to decide disputed points of Scripture.

Henry VIII now controlled the English Church as its supreme head. Yet why did bishops who held crucial votes in the House of Lords and Convocation permit the Henrician Reformation to occur? The answer is partly that Henry coerced his clerical opponents into submission by threats and punitive taxation; but some bishops actually *supported* the king, albeit sadly. They preferred to be ruled by the Tudors personally, with whom they could bargain and haggle, than be subordinated to Parliament, which was the alternative. As early as 1532 Cromwell had sought to make the Tudor supremacy parliamentary. But Parliament's contribution was cut back to the mechanical, though still revolutionary, task of enacting the requisite legislation. In Henry's view, the models for statecraft were the late Roman emperors, especially Constantine and Justinian, who governed both Church and State. Henry held his supremacy to be 'imperial' despite the use of Parliament. Royal supremacy was 'ordained by God'; all Parliament had done was belatedly to recognize the fact. Also it was not until 1549, 1552, and 1559 that the full implications of the break with Rome became clear, when the royal supremacy became the vehicle of the Protestant Reformation. Not everyone realized what was happening in the 1530s. Many saw the Acts of Appeals and Supremacy as a temporary squabble between king and pope, a cause unworthy of martyrdom.

Before 1529 Henry had ruled his clergy through Wolsey; after 1534 he did so personally, and through his second minister, Thomas Cromwell. A former aide of Wolsey, Cromwell had risen to power as a client of the Boleyn interest. By January 1532 he had taken command of the machinery of government, especially the management of Parliament. And by exploiting the offices of Master of the Jewels, King's Secretary, Lord Privy Seal, and Henry's (lay) vicegerent in spirituals, he became chief policymaker under Henry until he fell in June 1540. Indeed, some historians have argued that Cromwell was the architect of a Tudor 'revolution in government'. While this has never been proved, it remains true that he attempted the reform of the

King's Council and of Tudor financial institutions. In 1536 the large, unwieldy Council known to Henry VII and Wolsey was turned into an executive board of some nineteen persons and renamed the Privy Council. Forging ahead after 1540, the Privy Council made and enforced policy under the Crown, supervised the law courts, managed Exchequer finance, and co-ordinated the localities. Proceeding by state paper rather than royal writ, it became a partner of the Crown as much as a corporate servant. Cromwell's financial reforms also started to separate the financing of the royal family and household from that of national government, though this important process was not fully complete until the 1570s.

Yet Cromwell's major assignment was the Dissolution of the Monasteries. For three invincible forces merged after 1535 to dictate their removal. First, religious houses almost invariably owed allegiance to parent institutions outside England and Wales—this was juridically unacceptable after the Acts of Appeals and Supremacy. Secondly, Henry VIII was bankrupt. He needed to annex the monastic estates in order to restore the Crown's finances. Thirdly, Henry had to buy the allegiance of the political nation away from Rome and in support of his Reformation by massive injections of new patronage—he must appease the nobility and gentry with a share of the spoils. Thus Thomas Cromwell's first task as vicegerent was to conduct an ecclesiastical census under Henry's commission, the first major tax record since Domesday Book, to evaluate the condition and wealth of the English Church. Cromwell's questionnaire was a model of precision. Was divine service observed? Who were the benefactors? What lands did the houses possess? What rents?— and so on. The survey was completed in six months, and Cromwell's genius for administration was shown by the fact that *Valor Ecclesiasticus*, as it is known, served both as a record of the value of the monastic assets, and as a report on individual clerical incomes for taxation purposes.

The lesser monasteries were dissolved in 1536; the greater houses followed two years later. The process was interrupted by a formidable northern rebellion, the Pilgrimage of Grace, which was brutally crushed by use of martial law, exemplary public hangings, and a wholesale breaking of Henry's promises to the 'pilgrims'. But the work of plunder was quickly completed. A total of 560 monastic institutions had been suppressed by November 1539, and lands valued at £132,000 per annum immediately accrued to the Court of Augmentations of the King's Revenue, the new department of state set up by Cromwell to cope with the transfer of resources. Henry's coffers next received £75,000 or so from the sale of gold and silver plate, lead, and other precious items; finally, the monasteries had possessed the right of presentation to about two-fifths of the parochial benefices in England and Wales, and these rights were also added to the Crown's patronage.

The long-term effects of the dissolution have often been debated by historians, and may conveniently be divided into those which were planned, and those not. Within the former category, Henry VIII eliminated the last fortresses of potential resistance to his royal supremacy. He founded six new dioceses upon the remains of former monastic buildings and endowments—Peterborough, Gloucester, Oxford, Chester, Bristol, and Westminster, the last-named being abandoned in 1550. The king then reorganized the ex-monastic cathedrals as Cathedrals of the New Foundation, with revised staffs and statutes. Above all, though, the Crown's regular income was almost doubled—but for how long? The bitter irony of the dissolution was that Henry VIII's colossal military expenditure in the 1540s, together with the laity's demand for a share of the booty, politically irresistible as that was, would so drastically erode the financial gains as to cancel out the benefits of the entire process. Sales of the confiscated lands began even before the suppression of the greater houses was completed, and by 1547 almost two-thirds of the former monastic property had been alienated. Further grants by Edward VI and Queen Mary brought this figure to over three-quarters by 1558. The remaining lands were sold by Elizabeth I and the early Stuarts. It is true that the lands were not given away: out of 1,593 grants in Henry VIII's reign, only 69 were gifts or partly so; the bulk of grants (95.6 per cent) represented lands sold at prices based on fresh valuations. But the proceeds of sales were not invested— quite the opposite under Henry VIII. In any case, land *was* the best investment. The impact of sales upon the non-parliamentary income of the Crown was thus obvious, and there is something to be said for the view that it was Henry VIII's dissipation of the ex-monastic resources that made it difficult for his successors to govern England.

Of the unplanned effects of the dissolution, the wholesale destruction of fine Gothic buildings, melting down of medieval metalwork and jewellery, and sacking of libraries were acts of licensed vandalism. The clergy naturally suffered an immediate decline in morale. The number of candidates for ordination dropped sharply; there was little real conviction that Henry VIII's Reformation had anything to do with spiritual life, or with God. The disappearance of the abbots from the House of Lords meant that the ecclesiastical vote had withered away, leaving the laity ascendant in both Houses. With the sale of ex-monastic lands usually went the rights of parochial presentation attached to them, so that local laity obtained the bulk of Church patronage, setting the pattern for the next three centuries. The nobility and gentry, especially moderate-sized gentry families, were the ultimate beneficiaries of the Crown's land sales. The distribution of national wealth shifted between 1535 and 1558 overwhelmingly in favour of Crown and laity, as against the Church, and appreciably in favour of the nobility and gentry, as against the Crown. Very few new or substantially enlarged private estates were built up solely out of ex-monastic lands by 1558. But if Norfolk is a typical county, the changing pattern of wealth distribution at Elizabeth's accession was that 4.8 per cent of the county's manors were possessed by the Crown, 6.5 per cent were episcopal or other ecclesiastical manors, 11.4 per cent were owned by East Anglian territorial magnates, and 75.4 per cent had been acquired by the gentry. In 1535, 2.7 per cent of manors had been held by the Crown, 17.2 per cent had been owned by the monasteries, 9.4 per cent were in the hands of magnates, and 64 per cent belonged to gentry families.

Without Henry VIII's preparatory break with Rome, there could not have been Protestant reform in Edward VI's reign—thus evaluation can become a question of religious opinion, rather than historical judgement. However, it is hard not to regard Henry as a despoiler; he was scarcely a creator. Thomas Cromwell did his utmost, often behind the king's back, to endow his contemporaries with Erasmian, and enlightened, idealism: the Elizabethan Settlement owed much to the eirenic side of Cromwell's complex character. But Cromwell's reward was the block. When Henry became convinced that his vicegerent was protecting Protestants at Calais, he withdrew his support and allowed Cromwell to fall victim to his factional enemies. And without Wolsey or Cromwell to restrain him, Henry resolved to embark on French and Scottish wars, triggering a slow-burning fuse that was extinguished only by the execution of Mary Stuart in February 1587.

Yet if Henry turned to war and foreign policy in the final years of his reign, it was because he felt secure at last. Cromwell had provided the enforcement necessary to protect the supreme head from internal opposition; Jane Seymour had brought forth the male heir to the Tudor throne; Henry was excited about his marriage to Catherine Howard, and had settled Church doctrine by the Act of Six Articles (1539).

The matrimonial adventures of Henry VIII are too familiar to recount again in detail, but an outline may conveniently be given. Anne Boleyn was already pregnant when the king married her, and the future Elizabeth I was born on 7 September 1533. Henry was bitterly disappointed that she was not the expected son, and when Anne miscarried a deformed male foetus in January 1536, he was convinced that God had damned his second marriage. He therefore destroyed Anne in a palace coup (May 1536) and married Jane Seymour instead. But Jane's triumph in producing the baby Prince Edward was Pyrrhic, for she died of Tudor surgery twelve days later. Her successor was Anne of Cleves, whom Henry married in January 1540 to win European allies. But Anne, gentle but plain, did not suit; divorce was thus easy, as the union was never consummated. Catherine Howard came next. A high-spirited flirt, she had been a maid of honour to Anne of Cleves, and became Henry's fifth queen in July 1540, a month after the coup that destroyed Cromwell. She was executed in February 1542 for adultery. Finally, Henry took the amiable Catherine Parr to wife in July 1543. Twice widowed, Catherine was a cultivated Erasmian, who did much to preserve the cause of humanist reform until it could re-emerge in the reign of Edward VI.

Henry VIII's new plans for war, which hardened when he learned of Catherine Howard's infidelity, resurrected youthful dreams of French conquests. Wolsey had largely organized the king's early campaigns in 1512 and 1513; Henry led in person a large army from Calais in 1513, seizing Thérouanne and Tournai after the battle of the Spurs (16 August). True, the captured towns were costly to defend and Thomas Cromwell called them 'ungracious dogholes' in Parliament, but they delighted the king. Another invasion was planned, but Henry's allies were unreliable and Wolsey negotiated an Anglo-French *entente* (August 1514). This crumbled on the death of Louis XII and accession of Francis I (1 January 1515). But in 1518 Wolsey agreed new terms with France which were transformed into a dazzling European peace treaty. The pope, emperor, Spain, France, England, Scotland, Venice, Florence, and the Swiss forged, with others, a non-aggression pact with provision for mutual aid in case of hostilities. At a stroke Wolsey made London the centre of Europe and Henry VIII its arbiter. This *coup de théâtre* was the more remarkable in that it was the pope's own plan that Wolsey snatched from under his nose. At the Field of Cloth of Gold in 1520, Henry vied with Francis at a vast Renaissance tournament that was hailed as the eighth wonder of the world. Further campaigns in 1522 and 1523 brought Henry's army to within fifty miles of Paris. Then the best chance of all arose:

Henry's ally the Emperor Charles V defeated and captured Francis at the battle of Pavia (24 February 1525). But the opportunity could not be exploited owing to England's financial exhaustion. So Henry made peace with France. And when the divorce campaign began, he became insular in outlook, fearing Catholic invasion. Certainly he was in no position to resume warfare until the reverberations of the Pilgrimage of Grace had died away.

By 1541 Henry was moving towards a renewed amity with Spain against France, but he was prudent enough to hesitate. Tudor security required that, before England went to war with France, no doors should be open to the enemy within Britain itself. This meant an extension of English hegemony within the British Isles—Wales, Ireland, and Scotland. Accordingly Henry undertook, or continued, the wider task of English colonization that was completed by the Act of Union with Scotland (1707).

The Union of England and Wales had been presaged by Cromwell's reforming ambition, and was legally accomplished by Parliament in 1536 and 1543. The marcher lordships were shired, English laws and county administration were extended to Wales, and the shires and county boroughs were required to send twenty-four MPs to Parliament at Westminster. In addition, a refurbished Council of Wales, and new Courts of Great Sessions, were set up to administer the region's defences and judicial system. Wales was made subject to the full operation of royal writs, and to English principles of land tenure. The Act of 1543 dictated that Welsh customs of tenure and inheritance were to be phased out, and that English rules were to succeed them. Welsh customs persisted in remoter areas until the seventeenth century and beyond, but English customs soon predominated. English language became the fashionable tongue, and Welsh native arts went into decline.

Tudor Irish policy had begun with Henry VII's decision that acts of Parliament made in England were to apply to Ireland, and that the Irish Parliament could only legislate with the king of England's prior consent. By 1485 English authority did not in practice extend much beyond the Pale (the area around Dublin). But Ireland was generally quiet before 1534, even if the Gaelic chiefs held the balance of power. The Tudors ruled largely through the Anglo-Irish nobility before the Reformation, but a crisis erupted in 1533 when Irish politics began to merge with those of the Reformation. Surprised by the Kildare revolt (July 1534), Henry VIII could only parley with the rebels until a relief army was organized. Then the defeat of the rebels in August 1535 was followed by a major switch of policy: direct rule. For Cromwell's aim was to assimilate Ireland into the unitary realm of England under the control of an English-born deputy. Yet this policy required the backing of a standing army controlled from Westminster. Next, Henry VIII changed his style from 'lord' to 'king' of Ireland (June 1541). His assumption of the kingship was justified on the grounds that 'for lack of naming' of sovereignty the Irish had not been as obedient 'as they of right and according to their allegiance and bounden duties ought to have been'. But the move committed England to a possible full-scale conquest of Ireland, should the chiefs rebel, or should the Irish Reformation, begun by Cromwell, fail. It even militated *against* the idea of a unitary state. For a subordinate superstructure had been created for Ireland: the later Tudors ruled technically two separate kingdoms, each with its own bureaucracy. In future ideological terms, it became possible to conceive of Anglo-Irish nationalism, as opposed to English or Gaelic civilization. Lastly, despite the confiscation of Kildare's estates and the dissolution by Henry VIII of half the Irish monasteries, the Irish revenues were insufficient to maintain either the Crown's new royal status or its standing army. And since the army could not be withdrawn, the case for the conquest of Ireland was reinforced.

Yet the linchpin of Tudor security was the need to control Scotland. James IV (1488–1513) had renewed the Auld Alliance with France in 1492 and further provoked Henry VII by offering support for Perkin Warbeck. But the first of the Tudors declined to be distracted by Scottish sabre-rattling, and forged

The Principality of Wales 1284–1536
Boundary of Wales as subject to the jurisdiction of the Court of Great Sessions, 1542–1830
Boundary of Wales and the Border Counties subject to the Council of Wales
0 10 20 miles
0 10 20 30 km
ANGLESEY
Bangor
CAERNARVON
DENBIGH
FLINT
R. Dee
Chester
MERIONETH
FLINT
Shrewsbury
R. Severn
MONTGOMERY
SHROPSHIRE
Ludlow
RADNOR
WORCESTER
Worcester
CARDIGAN
HEREFORD
St Davids
CARMARTHEN
BRECKNOCK
Gloucester
PEMBROKE
MONMOUTH
GLOUCESTER
GLAMORGAN
Llandaff
R. Severn

THE UNION OF ENGLAND AND WALES

a treaty of Perpetual Peace with Scotland in 1502, followed a year later by the marriage of his daughter, Margaret, to King James. However, James tried to break the treaty shortly after Henry VIII's accession; Henry was on campaign in France, but sent the earl of Surrey northwards, and Surrey decimated the Scots at Flodden on 9 September 1513. The élite of Scotland—the king, three bishops, eleven earls, fifteen lords, and some 10,000 men—were slain in an attack that was the delayed acme of medieval aggression begun by Edward I and Edward III. The new Scottish king, James V, was an infant, and the English interest was symbolized by his mother, Henry VIII's own sister. But Scottish panic after Flodden had, if anything, confirmed the nation's ties with France, epitomized by the regency of John duke of Albany, who represented the French cause and urged Francis I to sponsor him in an invasion of England.

The French threat became overt when the mature James V visited France in 1536, and married in quick succession Madeleine, daughter of Francis I, and on her death Mary of Guise. In 1541 James agreed to meet Henry VIII at York, but committed the supreme offence of failing to turn up. By this time, Scotland was indeed a danger to Henry VIII, as its government was dominated by the French faction led by Cardinal Beaton, who symbolized both the Auld Alliance and the threat of papal counter-attack. In October 1542 the duke of Norfolk invaded Scotland, at first achieving little. It was the Scottish counterstroke that proved to be a worse disaster even than Flodden. On 24 November 1542, 3,000 English triumphed over 10,000 Scots at Solway Moss—and the news of the disgrace killed James V within a month. Scotland was left hostage to the fortune of Mary Stuart, a baby born only six days before James's death. For England, it seemed to be the answer to a prayer.

Henry VIII and Protector Somerset, who governed England during the early years of Edward VI's minority, none the less turned advantage into danger. Twin policies were espoused by which war with France was balanced by intervention in Scotland designed to secure England's back door. In 1543 Henry used the prisoners taken at Solway Moss as the nucleus of an English party in Scotland; he engineered Beaton's overthrow, and forced on the Scots the treaty of Greenwich, which projected union of the Crowns in form of marriage between Prince Edward and Mary Stuart. At the end of the same year, Henry allied with Spain against France, planning a combined invasion for the following spring. But the invasion, predictably, was not concerted. Henry was deluded by his capture of Boulogne; the emperor made a separate peace with France at Crépi, leaving England's flank exposed. At astronomical cost the war continued until June 1546. Francis I then finally agreed that England could keep Boulogne for eight years, when it was to be restored to France complete with expensive new fortifications. He also abandoned the Scots, endorsing by implication the terms of the treaty of Greenwich. But it was too late: Henry's 'rough wooing' of Scotland had already backfired. Beaton had trumped Henry's English party and repudiated the treaty; the earl of Hertford, the future Protector Somerset, was sent north with 12,000 men. Hertford's devastation of the border country, and Lothian, was successful, but was culpably counterproductive. In particular, the sack of Edinburgh united Scottish resistance to English terrorism. Henry VIII had thus engineered exactly what he wished to avoid—simultaneous conflict with France and Scotland. Hertford returned to Scotland in 1545, but the French faction remained ascendant, even after Beaton was murdered in May 1546 by a group of Fife lairds.

Edward VI

The death of Henry VIII in 1547, and the Protectorate until 1549 of the obsessional, vacillating Hertford as duke of Somerset left a power vacuum at the centre. This was paralleled locally by the temporary inability of county governments to contain outbreaks of violence and rebellion springing mainly from the decline in living standards in the 1540s. Riot and commotion were virtually ubiquitous from 1548 to 1550, save in the north where memories of the ill-fated Pilgrimage of Grace were perhaps still fresh. Coinage debasements designed to help pay for the French war had caused rampant inflation, and the most abrupt decline in the purchasing power of money coincided with Somerset's enclosure commissions and sheep tax, a platform that fermented rumours that the Protector supported the poor against the rich. The most serious uprisings took place in Devon and Cornwall, and in East Anglia, culminating in formal sieges of Exeter and Norwich by rebels. Somerset's equivocation, and inability to end this domestic crisis, prompted the earl of Warwick's coup against him in October 1549.

Yet Somerset's most spectacular failure was his continued adherence to the defunct treaty of Greenwich. His desire to realize Henry VIII's plan to subdue French influence in Scotland and achieve the union of the Crowns became an obsession. His victory at the battle of Pinkie (10 September 1547) was justified as an attempt to free Scotland from the Roman clergy, but the Scottish Reformation was hardly helped by a policy that pushed Scotland ever closer into the embrace of France. In June 1548, 6,000 French troops landed at Leith, and Mary Stuart was removed to France. When Somerset continued to threaten Scotland, Henry II of France declared war on England. Boulogne was blockaded; French forces in Scotland were strengthened. The Scots then agreed that Mary should eventually marry the Dauphin, heir to the French throne. That provision hammered the last nail into Somerset's coffin.

The earl of Warwick's coup, and realignment of the Privy Council, was completed by February 1550. Warwick shunned the title of Protector; instead he assumed that of Lord President of the Council, an interesting choice, since it revived an office effectively obsolete since the fall of Edmund Dudley, Warwick's father. Posthumous tradition has vilified Warwick as an evil schemer—a true 'Machiavel'. But it is hard to see why, for expediency in the interests of stability was the most familiar touchstone of Tudor policy. Three episodes allegedly prove Warwick's criminal cunning: his original coup against Somerset, the subsequent trial which ended in Somerset's execution in January 1552, and the notorious scheme to alter the succession to the throne in favour of Lady Jane Grey, Warwick's daughter-in-law. However, only the last of these charges seems justifiable by Tudor standards, and even this would be regarded differently by historians had the plot to exclude the Catholic Mary actually succeeded.

Warwick, who created himself duke of Northumberland in October 1551, made, in fact, a laudable effort to reverse the destabilization permitted, or left unchecked, by Somerset. Domestic peace was restored by the use of forces which included foreign mercenaries; England's finances were put back on course by means of enlightened reforms and retrenchments. Above all, Somerset's disastrous wars with France and Scotland were quickly terminated. Northumberland sought peace with dishonour—a humiliating but attractive alternative to fighting. Boulogne was returned to France at once; English garrisons in Scotland were withdrawn, and the treaty of Greenwich was quietly forgotten. It thus became inevitable that Mary Stuart would marry the Dauphin, but considerations of age ensured that the union was postponed until April 1558.

The English Reformation had meanwhile reached its crossroads. After Thomas Cromwell's execution, Henry VIII had governed the Church of England himself: his doctrinal conservatism was inflexible to the last. But Somerset rose to the Protectorate as leader of the Protestant faction in the Privy Council, and the young Edward VI—he was nine years old in 1547—mysteriously became a precocious and bigoted Protestant too. In July 1547, Somerset reissued Cromwell's Erasmian injunctions to the clergy, followed by a Book of Homilies, or specimen sermons, which embodied Protestant doctrines. He summoned Parliament four months later, and the Henrician doctrinal legislation was repealed. At the same time, the chantries were dissolved. These minor foundations existed to sing masses for the souls of their benefactors; as such, they encouraged beliefs in purgatory and the merits of requiems, doctrines which Protestants denied. Somerset thus justified their abolition on religious grounds, but it is plain that he coveted their property even more to finance his Scottish ambitions. Next, the Privy Council wrote to Archbishop Cranmer, ordering the wholesale removal of images from places of worship, 'images which be things not necessary, and without which the churches of Christ continued most godly many years'. Shrines, and the jewels and plate inside them, were promptly seized by the Crown; the statues and wall-paintings that decorated English parish churches were mutilated, or covered with whitewash. In 1538 Henry VIII had suppressed shrines which were centres of pilgrimages, notably that of St. Thomas Becket at Canterbury. Protector Somerset finalized the destruction already begun, ensuring that the native art, sculpture, metalwork, and embroidery associated with Catholic ritual were comprehensively wiped out.

The danger was always that Protestant reform would overreach itself—in the Cornish rebellion of 1549, opposition to the first of Cranmer's Prayer Books provided the chief rallying point. The system for licensing public preachers had broken down by September 1548, and Somerset was obliged, temporarily, to ban all preaching, whether licensed or not, in favour of readings of the official homilies. The Protector, though, promised 'an end of all controversies in religion' and 'uniform order', and Cranmer also aspired to this ideal. He wrote to Albert Hardenberg, leader of the Bremen Reformed Church:

We are desirous of setting forth in our churches the true doctrine of God, neither have we any wish to be shifting and unstable, or to deal in ambiguities: but, laying aside all carnal considerations, to transmit to posterity a true and explicit form of doctrine agreeable to the rule of the scriptures; so that there may be set forth among all nations a testimony respecting our doctrine, delivered by the grave authority of learned and pious men; and that all posterity may have a pattern which they may imitate. For the purpose of carrying this important design into effect we have thought it necessary to have the assistance of learned men, who, having compared their opinions together with us, may do away with doctrinal controversies, and establish an entire system of true doctrine.

Protestant theologians who responded to Cranmer's call included John Knox from Scotland, Martin Bucer from Strasbourg, John à Lasco from Poland, Peter Martyr Vermigli from Italy, and Bernardino Ochino, the controversial ex-vicargeneral of the Capuchins, who had made a sensational conversion to Protestantism in the early 1540s.

Yet Protestants were even less capable of consensus than were Catholics. John Knox, to whom Northumberland inadvertently offered the bishopric of Rochester (fortunately Knox refused), was particularly atavistic; he thrived on crisis. Cranmer soon came to see that unity could only be achieved at the price of uniformity—this was the fundamental lesson of the English Reformation. Accordingly the two editions of his Book of Common Prayer (1549, 1552), which enshrined the pure and Scriptural doctrines for which the primate had craved since 1537, not only had to be approved by Parliament; they had to be enforced by Acts of Uniformity. The advantages from Cranmer's viewpoint were that the Books were in English, and the second was unambiguously Protestant; the drawback was that the Prayer Books were first published as schedules to the Uniformity Acts, so that the doctrines and ceremonies of the English Church now rested on parliamentary authority, rather than on the independent legislative power of the supreme head. This constitutional amendment marked the final triumph of the Tudor laity over the Church, for Elizabeth I, in fashioning the religious settlement of 1558–9, took Cranmer's Prayer Books as a precedent.

Queen Mary

Northumberland's patronage of Knox, who in exile during Mary's reign scandalized Europe by theorizing upon the rights of subjects to rebel against idolatrous rulers, illustrates how far the duke had linked his future to the Protestant cause. Edward VI had never enjoyed good health, and by the late spring of 1553 it was plain that he was dying. By right of birth, as well as under Henry VIII's will, Mary, Catherine of Aragon's Catholic daughter, was the lawful successor. But Northumberland's attempted *putsch* in July 1553 needs more than a casual explanation. The facts are that Northumberland bound his family to the throne on 21 May by marrying his eldest son to Lady Jane Grey. Jane was the eldest daughter of the marquis of Dorset, and residuary legatee of the Crown, after the Princesses Mary and Elizabeth, under Henry VIII's will. Next, a documentary 'device' was drafted, by which Edward VI disinherited his sisters and bequeathed his throne to Jane and her heirs. Edward died on 6 July 1553; Northumberland and the Council proclaimed Jane queen four days later. The duke's treachery seems proved. Yet the plot may have been Edward's. The Protestant boy-bigot hated his sisters, especially Mary; the 'device' was drafted in his own hand, and corrected by him. At the very least, Edward had been Northumberland's willing collaborator.

Jane Grey ruled for nine days. Knox preached on her behalf, and threatened popery and tyranny should Mary enforce her claim. But the *putsch* was doomed. Mary was allowed to escape to Framlingham, the walled fortress of the Catholic Howard family. Proclaimed by the East Anglian gentry, she marched south. London changed sides; Northumberland, Jane, and their principal adherents eventually went to the block.

Yet Mary triumphed because she cheated. The Norfolk gentry were persuaded of her Tudor legitimism; they learned the terrible extent of her Catholicism only after she was safely enthroned at Westminster. Even so, we should beware of the bias of John Foxe and other Protestant polemicists writing in Elizabeth's reign, who would prefer us to believe that Mary did nothing but persecute. It is true that Mary burned a minimum of 287 persons after February 1555, and others died in prison. But the leading Protestant martyrs, Bishops Hooper, Ridley, Latimer, and Archbishop Cranmer were as much the victims of straightforward political vengeance. Stephen Gardiner, the failed conservative manipulator of Henry VIII's reign, who had been outwitted by Thomas Cromwell in the 1530s, was abandoned by the king in the 1540s, and had languished in the Tower during Edward's reign, had become Lord Chancellor in 1553; he had bitter scores to settle. Secondly, we should appreciate that many of the Marian 'martyrs' would have been burnt as anabaptists, or Lollards, under Henry VIII. By sixteenth-century standards there was nothing exceptional about Mary's reign of terror beyond the fact that, as in the case of More when he had persecuted Protestants as Lord Chancellor, she regarded her work as well done. Even the scale of Mary's persecution may have been exaggerated, for the figures come from the biased Foxe, who reported the same examples twice whenever possible, and who conveniently forgot that the un-persecuted Lollards of Edward's reign had created a backlog.

Mary's true goal was always England's reunion with Rome; persecution was a minor aspect of her programme. It was thus to her advantage that the parliamentary landed laity were, by this date, thoroughly secular-minded, for they repealed the Henrician and Edwardian religious legislation almost without comment, and re-enacted the heresy laws—all the time their sole condition was that the Church lands taken since 1536 should not be restored. Yet Mary needed papal assistance; she could not work alone. In November 1554, Cardinal Pole, an English Catholic exile of Plantagenet lineage, landed in England, absolved the kingdom from sin, and proclaimed papal reunion. Pole, who was appointed Archbishop of Canterbury, then attempted to implement intelligent ecclesiastical reforms in the spirit of the Counter-Reformation: these covered such areas as the liturgy, clerical manners, education, and episcopal super-vision. But Pole's approach was visionary. He saw people not as individuals but as a multitude; he emphasized discipline before preaching; and he sought to be an 'indulgent' pastor who relieved his flock of choices they were too foolish to make for themselves. Yet heresy could not be contained by such methods. Dubbing himself the 'Pole Star', Pole thought his mere presence could guide lost souls. And he was afforded neither the time nor the money needed to accomplish his tasks: three years, and virtually no money, were not enough. The ecclesiast-ical machine ground slowly; standards of clerical education could not be raised without the augmentation of stipends, espe-cially in the north.

Mary's short reign was, nevertheless, surprisingly successful in other spheres. The financial reforms of Northumberland were completed; the Exchequer was revitalized and reorgan-ized; a blueprint for recoinage was prepared, and was adopted under Elizabeth. In 1557, a committee was named to investigate 'why customs and subsidies be greatly diminished and decayed'.

The outcome was a new Book of Rates in May 1558, which increased customs receipts by 75 per cent. Nothing on this scale would be tried again until James I's reign, when the Great Contract of 1610 proved such a disastrous failure.

Yet Mary made two bad mistakes. The first was to allow some 800 English Protestants to emigrate to Frankfurt, Zurich, and Geneva. For not only did these exiles launch a relentless crusade of anti-Catholic propaganda and subversive literature against England, which the government was obliged to suppress or refute as best it could; they also flocked home again upon the accession, in 1558, of Elizabeth, the Protestant Deborah, as they believed her to be, when some were appointed bishops, despite the inherent tension between the Anglican ceremonials they became obliged to enforce, and the Genevan distaste for popish rituals and vestments they had so recently shared. Mary's second mistake was her Spanish marriage. Her union with Philip, son of the Emperor Charles V, was her own idea, celebrated in July 1554 despite the pleas of privy councillors and Parliament. Philip was styled king jointly with Mary as queen during her lifetime; however, his rights in England were to expire if Mary died childless, as proved to be the case. Yet even these terms did not appease opponents of the match: four simultaneous rebellions were planned for 1554, of which Sir Thomas Wyatt's, in Kent, began prematurely in January. Wyatt led 3,000 men to London, proclaiming that 'we seek no harm to the Queen, but better council and counsellors'. But Wyatt declined to pillage London; he removed his force to Kingston—a fatal diversion. His army was defeated, and 100 rebels, including Wyatt, were executed as traitors. The other projected rebellions came to nothing.

Wyatt's fear that England would become a Spanish pawn was, none the less, justified. In 1556, Philip became king of Spain, following Charles V's abdication. Within a year, he had dragged his wife into a war with Henry II of France, which culminated in the recapture of Calais by the duke of Guise (7 January 1558). Calais, apart from its commercial value as the wool Staple, was symbolic of the glorious French campaigns of the Black Prince and Henry V: its loss was more than bad luck. Mary's death in November 1558 was thus unmourned, and the fact that Cardinal Pole died within a few hours of the queen was a positive fillip. Henry II meanwhile exulted with Te Deum and bonfires, and the marriage of Mary Stuart to the Dauphin, the perilous consequence of the aggression of Henry VIII and Somerset, was expedited.

Elizabeth I

Elizabeth I, daughter of Henry VIII and Anne Boleyn, ascended her throne on 17 November 1558. Ruler of England for forty-four years, she has won a reputation far in excess of her achievements. It is plain that her own propaganda, the cult of Gloriana, her sheer longevity, the coincidence of the Shakespearian moment, and the defeat of the Armada have beguiled us into ignoring the many problems of her reign.

Yet whatever fables have been peddled, Sir Robert Naunton was right when he said: 'Though very capable of counsel, she was absolute enough in her own resolution, which was apparent even to her last.' She knew her mind and controlled her policy; her instinct to power was infallible. Councillors attempted to concert their approaches to her on sensitive matters, but they were rarely successful; she would lose her temper whereupon the matter would rest in abeyance. But she postponed important decisions: unless panicked, she could delay for years. On the other hand, her attitude has to be offset against her financial position and the conservatism of most of her subjects who were far from being Protestant 'converts' before the outbreak of war with Spain. Possibly her greatest asset was *lack* of preconceptions; she was not a conviction-politician like Sir Francis Walsingham or the earl of Leicester, though her taste for *realpolitik* exceeded Lord Burghley's. Apart from her concern to recover Calais as revealed by her French campaign of 1563, she ignored conventional royal ambitions. Her father's expansionist dreams were absent; her sister's ideological passions were eschewed; and despite negotiations conducted until 1582, a dynastic marriage was avoided. For although the second half of the sixteenth century saw the rise of ideological coalitions in Europe, England did not possess sufficient resources to wage open war until the 1580s; therefore a passive stance that responded to events as they occurred, while shunning obvious initiatives, was appropriate.

At first, though, the emphasis was on religious settlement. The efforts of Northumberland and Mary to reverse the destabilization of 1547–9 were flatly contradictory. Hence Elizabeth's coronation slogan was 'concord'. Her personal *credo* remains elusive, but she may originally have aimed to revive Henry VIII's religious legislation, to re-establish her royal supremacy and the break with Rome, and to permit communion in both kinds (bread and wine) after the reformed fashion— but nothing else. If so, she was 'bounced' by her chief councillor, William Cecil, for the only time in her reign. For when Parliament assembled in January 1559, he introduced bills to re-establish royal supremacy and full Protestant worship based on the 1552 Prayer Book. And when these were opposed by the Marian bishops and conservative peers, he baited a trap for the Catholics. A disputation was begun at Westminster Abbey (31 March) which restricted debate to what was justified by Scripture alone. When the Catholics walked out, Cecil had a propaganda victory: two bishops were even imprisoned. True, Elizabeth was styled 'supreme governor' of the English Church in an effort to minimize the impact of the supremacy. But when the Acts of Supremacy and Uniformity finally passed, they did so without a single churchman's consent, thereby making constitutional history. The cry of 'foul' was taken up by Catholic apologists, who accused Cecil of coercion 'partly by violence and partly by fear'. And another act returned to the Crown such ex-monastic property as Mary at her own expense had begun to restore to the Church, while a final act strengthened the Crown's estates at the expense of the bishops. The Elizabethan Settlement was completed in 1563, when Convocation approved Thirty-nine Articles defining the Anglican Church's doctrine—these were based on forty-two articles drafted by Cranmer in Edward VI's reign. Lastly, in 1571, the Settlement gained teeth sharper than the Act of Uniformity, when a Subscription Act required the beneficed clergy to assent to the Thirty-nine Articles.

The Anglican Church eventually became a pillar of the Elizabethan state. Despite its faults, the framework that John Jewel defended in his *Apology of the Church of England* (1562), and to which the 'judicious' Richard Hooker gave rational credibility in *The Laws of Ecclesiastical Polity* (1594–1600), the 'Church by law Established' saved England from the religious civil war that afflicted other European countries at the time, notably France. Yet while the Settlement meant that England became officially Protestant in 1559, a huge missionary effort to win the hearts and minds of parishioners (especially those in remoter counties and borderlands) lay ahead. Outside London, the South East, parts of East Anglia, and towns such as Bristol, Coventry, Colchester and Ipswich, Catholicism predominated at Elizabeth's accession: the bishops and most parochial incumbents were Marians, and committed Protestants were few. Whereas Elizabeth and Cecil inherited all the negative and destructive elements of Henrician anti-papalism and Edwardian Protestantism, they had inadequate resources to build the Anglican Church, though it is false to see their task purely in confessional terms. For by this stage, inertia was strong among those who had come to regard the Church as a rich corporation to be asset-stripped, or as a socio-political nexus whose leaders were local governors and whose festivals characterized the communal year. In addition, Protestantism, with its emphasis on 'godly' preaching and Bible study, was an academic creed, unattractive to illiterate villagers steeped in the oral traditions and symbolic ritualism of medieval England.

The decline of Catholicism in the parishes during Elizabeth's reign was due partly to its own internal changes and partly to the success of committed Protestants in marketing a rival evangelical product. One dynamic change sprang from mortality.

For the post-Reformation English Catholic community owed everything to Henrician and Marian survivalism, and relatively little to the missions of seminary priests and Jesuits after 1570. Over 225 Marian priests who saw themselves as Roman Catholics and who had separated from the Anglican Church were active in Yorkshire and Lancashire before 1571, supported by a fifth column within the official Church that remained willing to propagandize for Rome. By 1590, however, barely a quarter of the Marian clergy were still alive, and no more than a dozen by 1603. It is important not to forget the conditions in which the Catholics had to work. The penal laws became savage as fears of Spanish invasion increased. In 1584–5, Parliament enacted that if a priest had been ordained by papal authority since 1559, no additional proof was needed to convict him of treason. Furthermore, 123 of the 146 priests executed between the passing of this act and Elizabeth's death were indicted under its terms, and not under those of earlier treason laws. But it was the challenge of Anglicanism, rather than the threat of persecution, that succeeded in forcing Catholicism into minority status. Protestant evangelism was largely based on preaching, though Elizabeth's personal views and lack of resources precluded a full government programme for the propagation of Protestant preaching. What was achieved was often due to voluntary 'puritan' efforts. For whereas under Henry VIII and Edward VI the impetus for the Reformation had come largely from the regime, under Elizabeth, by contrast, the 'primary thrust' of Protestant evangelism came from below.

A term of abuse, 'puritan' was used to index the nature and extent of opinions of which conservatives disapproved. It meant a 'church rebel' or 'hotter sort' of Protestant; but the core of puritanism lay in the capacity of 'godly' Protestants to recognize each other within a corrupt and unregenerate world. Men of conviction, many of them former Marian exiles, the 'puritans' sought to extirpate corruption and 'popish rituals' from the Church (the cross in baptism, kneeling at the Communion, wearing of copes and surplices, the use of organs, etc.), but

Elizabeth consistently refused to adjust the Settlement even in detail. The most she was prepared to do was to refer petitions of which she approved to the bishops. In fact, when points were tested by puritan clergy, strict conformity was required. Archbishop Parker's *Advertisements* (1566), issued in response to disputes over clerical dress and ceremonies, enforced the rubrics of the Prayer Book. And when Edmund Grindal (Archbishop of Canterbury, 1576–83), who shared the puritan desire for reformation, dared to tell Elizabeth he was subject to a higher power, he was suspended from office. His successor, John Whitgift (1583–1604), required all clergy to subscribe to the royal supremacy, Prayer Book, and Thirty-nine Articles, or else be deprived.

Yet the need to graft the Anglican Church into English national consciousness was only the first of several tests faced by the regime. In April 1559, the peace of Cateau-Cambrésis (between Spain, France, and England) ended Mary's French war and Philip II briefly joined the queue of suitors for Elizabeth's hand. During the 1560s, Spain sought to preserve the amity with England, not least to ensure free traffic through the English Channel to the Spanish Netherlands. Yet Catholics, the papacy, Spain, and France were potential foes: the real danger was the threat of a Catholic coalition against England. And by 1569 the Catholic cause was linked to intrigue which, in its more innocent variety, sought to recognize Mary Stuart's right as Elizabeth's successor, but in more dangerous forms plotted to depose Elizabeth and enthrone Mary.

Mary had married the Dauphin in April 1558, and seven months later the Scottish Parliament agreed to offer him the crown matrimonial in exchange for support for the Scottish Reformation. Mary Tudor's death unleashed new French intervention in Scotland; there was sporadic fighting, which was overtaken by full-blooded Protestant revolution. When John Knox returned from exile in Geneva to preach at Perth in May 1559, he lit the fuse of a delayed explosion. Mary Stuart's husband succeeded to the French throne as Francis II in July

1559, but when he died in December 1560 the Scottish queen was forced to return to Edinburgh—she was back by August 1561. By then Elizabeth and Cecil had intervened on Knox's side: the Scottish Reformation had become the vehicle for the expulsion of Continental influence from the British Isles, and the assertion of the hegemony sought by Henry VIII.

Elizabeth meanwhile declined to marry or name her successor. Her obstinacy drove Cecil and the Privy Council to distraction. By contrast Mary Stuart's supporters hoped that she would succeed Elizabeth in a Catholic coup. For Mary's grandmother had been Henry VIII's sister, Margaret. But Mary made mistakes in Scotland; she alienated her friends as well as enemies, lost the battle of Langside, and fled to England in May 1568. Elizabeth, in effect, imprisoned her. A chain of intrigues took shape, in which Catholic, papal, and pro-Spanish ambitions allied, threateningly, with anti-Cecil factionalism at Court. But the Northern Rising of 1569, led by the disillusioned Catholic earls of Northumberland and Westmorland, was incoherently attempted and easily crushed. By 1572, Elizabeth and Cecil had passed another major test. Stability had been preserved: Cecil was ennobled as Lord Burghley.

The Northern Rising and Mary's imprisonment began a new phase in Tudor politics. Throughout Europe, opinion was polarizing on religious grounds: England's role as a Protestant champion was highlighted. Relations with Spain deteriorated when Cecil seized Philip II's treasure-ships *en route* for the Netherlands (December 1568). Then Pope Pius V issued a bull, *Regnans in Excelsis* (February 1570), that declared Elizabeth excommunicated and urged loyal Catholics to depose her. There followed the massacre of Protestants in Paris on St. Bartholomew's Day 1572 and outright revolt in the Netherlands—both fired Protestant consciences and inspired Englishmen to volunteer aid to the Netherlands. Lastly, Elizabeth's *entente* with France as a counter against Spain, which was twice taken to the point of marriage negotiations, was regarded as hostile by Philip II. On these matters the Privy

Council was divided. But these divisions were not pro- and anti-Spanish but between *realpolitik* and religion. With few exceptions, members of the Privy Council were united against Spain and committed to the European Protestant cause. In particular, Burghley, the earl of Sussex, Leicester, and Walsingham agreed on the broad aims of a Protestant foreign policy in the 1570s and 1580s. Their differences centred only on the extent to which England should become militarily committed. For Leicester and Walsingham wanted direct English intervention in the Netherlands, but the queen and Burghley were adamant that England alone could not survive war with Spain.

Yet when war with Spain came in 1585, England was isolated. After 1572 Elizabeth assisted France against Spain in the Netherlands, trying to reconcile conflicting political, religious, and commercial interests at minimum cost. She backed Francis duke of Anjou, her most plausible suitor, brother and heir of Henry III of France. But Anjou died in June 1584 having failed to halt Spanish recovery in the Low Countries. And since the Protestant Henry of Navarre now became heir to the French throne, the Wars of Religion resumed in France: the Guise Court party allied with Spain (secret treaty of Joinville, December 1584). So France was divided while Philip II prospered. He annexed Portugal (1580) and the Azores (1582–3): the size of his combined fleets exceeded those of the Netherlands and England combined. At this point the Marquis of Santa Cruz proposed the 'Enterprise of England'—an Armada to overthrow Elizabeth. Observers debated only whether the Netherlands or England would be reduced first.

The pivotal event was the assassination of the Dutch leader, William of Orange (10 July 1584). This created panic among English politicians who feared that Elizabeth, too, might fall victim. In May 1585, Philip felt confident enough to seize all English ships in Iberian ports; Elizabeth responded by giving Leicester his head, allying with the Dutch States General in August, and dispatching the earl to Holland with an army. But Leicester's mission was a fiasco; his ignominious return in

December 1587 was shortly followed by his death. Only Sir Francis Drake and other naval freebooters enjoyed success. And outright war followed Mary Stuart's execution in February 1587. For new Catholic plots, at least one of which involved Elizabeth's attempted assassination, hardened the Privy Council's attitude. Elizabeth stood indecisive and immobile; Mary had been tried and convicted, but she was of the royal blood. But the Council could wait no longer: the sentence was put into effect. Scotland fulminated, but the twenty-one-year-old James VI was appeased by subsidies and enhanced prospects of the greatest of glittering prizes—succession to the English Crown. (In any case, James had no illusions about Spanish support for the Scottish Reformation.)

The Armada was sighted off the Scilly Isles on 19 July 1588: the objective was the conquest of England, which would itself assure the reconquest of the Netherlands. Philip's plan was to win control of the English Channel, to rendezvous with the duke of Parma off the coast of Holland, and to transport the crack troops of Philip's Army of Flanders to England. The main fleet was to cover Parma's crossing, and then unite forces carried by the Armada itself with Parma's army in a combined invasion of England. The Armada was commanded by the duke of Medina Sidonia; the English fleet was led by Lord Howard of Effingham, with Drake as second in command. Effingham sailed in the *Ark Royal*, built for Sir Walter Raleigh in 1581; Drake captained the *Revenge*, commissioned in 1575. In England the local militias were mobilized; possible landing places were mapped, and their defences strengthened. But had Parma landed, his army would have decimated English resistance: the effectiveness of English sea-power was vital.

In the event, the defeat of the Armada was not far removed from traditional legend, romantic games of bowls excepted. The key to the battle was artillery: the Armada carried only 19 or 20 full cannon and its 173 medium-heavy and medium guns were ineffective—some exploded on use which suggests that they were untested. And whereas the Spanish had only 21 culverins (long-range iron guns), the English had 153; whereas the Spanish had 151 demi-culverins, the English had 344. In brief, Effingham and Drake outsailed and outgunned their opponents. The battered Armada fled north towards the Firth of Forth, trailing back to Spain via the Orkneys and the west coast of Ireland. In August 1588 Protestant England celebrated with prayers and public thanksgiving. But the escape was narrow; Elizabeth never again committed her whole fleet in battle at once. Moreover, although later generations boasted that she kept Spain at bay at minimum cost by avoiding foreign alliances and relying on the royal navy and part-time privateers who preyed on enemy shipping, the supremacy of the naval over the Continental land war is a myth. The war at sea was only part of a struggle that gripped the whole of western Europe and centred on the French civil war and revolt of the Netherlands. Since Elizabeth lacked the land forces, money, and manpower to rival Spain, she was obliged to help Navarre and the Dutch. The Catholic League was strongest in Picardy, Normandy, and Brittany; these regions and the Netherlands formed what amounted to a continuous war zone. Elizabeth dispatched auxiliary forces annually to France and the Netherlands in 1589–95; cash subsidies apart from the cost of equipping and paying these troops cost her over £1 million. By comparison, English naval operations were heroic sideshows of mixed strategic value.

Yet late Elizabethan policy was damaging from several viewpoints. For the aims of Navarre and his partners diverged, and when in July 1593 he converted to Catholicism to secure his throne as Henry IV, he soured hopes of a European Protestant coalition. Elizabeth, however, continued to support him, since a united France restored the balance of power in Europe, while his debts ensured continued Anglo-French collaboration in the short term. Next, the queen quarrelled with the Dutch over their mounting debts and the cost of English garrisons and auxiliary forces. Thirdly, the cost of the war was unprecedented in English history: even with parliamentary subsidies, it could only be met by borrowing and by sales of Crown lands. Lastly, the war, in effect, spread to Ireland. The Irish Reformation had not succeeded: Spanish invasions as dangerous as the Armada were attempted there. These, combined with serious internal revolt, obliged the Privy Council to think in terms of the full-scale conquest of Ireland logically induced by Henry VIII's assumption of the kingship. Elizabeth hesitated—as well she might. At last her favourite, the dazzling but paranoid earl of Essex, was dispatched in 1599 with a large army. But Essex's failure surpassed even Leicester's in the Netherlands; he deserted his post in a last-ditch attempt to salvage his career by personal magnetism, and was executed in February 1601 for leading his faction in a desperate rebellion through the streets of London. Lord Mountjoy replaced him in Ireland, reducing the Gaelic chiefs to submission and routing a Spanish invasion force in 1601. The conquest of Ireland was completed by 1603. Yet the results were inherently contradictory: English hegemony was confirmed, but the very fact of conquest alienated the indigenous population and vanquished hopes of advancing the Irish Reformation, and thus achieving cultural unity with England.

Such contradictions were not, however, confined to Irish history. Internal tension became inexorably pronounced in Elizabethan government and society. If the English Deborah had constructed the Anglican Church, thwarted rebellion, defeated the Armada, and pacified Ireland, the Tudor stability thus restored, and preserved, was none the less vulnerable to structural decay. Problems that were at first relatively minor gained momentum as the reign progressed, but the queen's caution and immobility prevented her from taking remedial action in time. It was as if the sheer effort of making the Settlement of 1559 had sapped away Elizabeth's creative powers, or perhaps the extent to which she had been pushed into Protestantism then had dissuaded her from permitting further changes in any sphere. Perhaps she was simply too much her father's daughter? In any event, her constancy, so admired in her youth, deteriorated with age into indecisiveness, inertia, and benign neglect.

The most obvious area of decline was that of government.

Did Elizabethan institutions succumb to decay during the war with Spain? Criticism centres on the inadequacy of taxation, local government, and military recruitment; an alleged 'slide to disaster' in the provinces caused by alienation of less exalted 'country' gentlemen from the Court; the rise of corruption in central administration; the abuse of royal prerogative to grant lucrative 'monopolies' or licences in favour of courtiers and their clients, who might also enforce certain statutes for profit; and the claim that the benefits of the Poor Laws were negligible in relation to the rise in population and scale of economic distress in the 1590s.

It is true, Elizabeth and Burghley allowed the taxation system to decline. Not only did the value of a parliamentary subsidy fail to increase in line with inflation despite soaring levels of government expenditure, but receipts dropped in cash terms owing to static tax assessments and widespread evasion. Rates became stereotyped, while the basis of assessment became the taxpayer's unsworn declaration. And whereas Wolsey had attempted to tax wage-earners as well as landowners in Henry VIII's reign, Elizabeth largely abandoned the effort. Although the yield of a subsidy was £140,000 at the beginning of Elizabeth's reign, it was only £80,000 at the end. In Sussex, the average tax assessment of seventy leading families fell from £61 in the 1540s to £14 by the 1620s; and some potential taxpayers escaped altogether. In Suffolk 17,000 taxpayers were assessed for the subsidy of 1523 but only 7,700 for that of 1566. True, the Privy Council ordered subsidy commissioners to ensure that assessments were made impartially and 'answerable to the meaning of Parliament' and 'not so underfoot as heretofore hath been used'. Yet Burghley himself evaded tax, despite holding office as Lord Treasurer after 1572. He grumbled hypocritically in Parliament about tax cheating, but kept his own assessment of income static at £133. 6s. 8d.—his real income was approximately £4,000 per annum. Lord North admitted that few taxpayers were assessed at more than one-sixth or one-tenth of their true wealth, 'and many be 20 times, some 30, and some much more worth than they be set at, which the commissioner cannot without oath help'. And when arguing in Parliament for exemption of lesser taxpayers in 1601, Raleigh suggested that while the wealth of a person valued in the subsidy books at £3 per annum was close to his true worth, 'our estates that be £30 or £40 in the Queen's books are not the hundredth part of our wealth'.

The initiative, however, had to come from the Crown. And the striking feature of Elizabeth's strategy is that while elsewhere European rulers were inventing new taxes under the pressure of war or threat of invasion, Elizabeth stuck to precedent. She resisted fiscal innovation, extracting some three per cent of England's national income for the war, whereas Philip II appropriated 10 per cent of Castile's. She exacted multiple subsidies after 1589, but these were subject to the law of diminishing returns: the same few taxpayers were assessed using the same stereotyped valuations, though not even the humblest taxpayer was charged at modern rates of income tax.

The failure of Elizabethan government to maintain the yield of the subsidy was the biggest weakness of the late-Tudor state. Yet Elizabeth left an accumulated debt of only £365,000. Since Mary had left a debt of £300,000, the comparison (allowing for inflation) is entirely to her sister's credit. Within six years James I had paid all but £133,500 of this debt, though his own deficits dwarfed anything envisaged by Elizabeth. But Elizabeth bridged the gap between receipts and expenditure by sales of Crown land and borrowing. Lands worth £267,800 were sold between 1560 and 1574, and £608,000 was raised from land sales between 1589 and 1603. Also £461,500 was borrowed during the war with Spain. Such expedients reduced future revenue and deprived the Crown of security against loans. Yet how many early-modern rulers took a long-term view, especially in wartime? It is easy to accuse Elizabeth of mismanagement, but we tend to forget that she was not accountable to an electorate.

Another point to note is that local taxation escalated under Elizabeth, especially for poor relief, road and bridge repairs, and militia expenditure, all of which compensated to some extent for the inadequacy of national taxation. Although this subject is relatively unexplored, it is clear that the recruitment and training of the militia was very expensive and burdened the localities with additional rates which were authorized by Justices of the Peace and collected by hundred and parish constables. Training cost considerable sums by the 1580s; the localities were responsible, too, for providing stocks of parish arms and armour; for paying muster-masters; for repairing coastal forts and building beacons; and for issuing troops mustered for the foreign service with weapons and uniforms, as well as conveying them to the required port of embarkation. In Kent the cost of military preparations borne by the county between 1585 and 1603 exceeded £10,000. True, a proportion of 'coat-and-conduct' money required to equip and transport troops was recoverable from the Exchequer, but in practice the localities met roughly three-quarters of the cost. Also whereas merchant ships (except customarily fishing vessels) had traditionally been requisitioned from coastal towns and counties to augment the royal navy in time of war, the Crown in the 1590s started demanding money as well as ships, and impressed fishermen for service in the royal navy and aboard privateers to the detriment of the local economy. And when the ship money rate was extended to inland areas such as the West Riding of Yorkshire, it aroused opposition to the point where the Crown's right to impose it was questioned.

While, however, the needs and agencies of defence, military recruitment, and finance assumed prominence in Elizabethan government, the backbone of the system remained the local magistracy. The key officials were unsalaried JPs, whose numbers increased from on average fewer than ten for each county in 1500, to forty or fifty by the middle of Elizabeth's reign, and up to ninety by 1603. But the main Tudor innovation in local government was the lieutenancy system made permanent in 1585. Whereas earlier appointments had been temporary, designed to subordinate the shire levies to a single official, the outbreak of war with Spain prompted a new departure. Lieutenancy commissions were issued for nearly all the English and Welsh counties, and the length of the war meant that in many cases the appointees continued in post for life. In general, the lord-lieutenant was the senior resident nobleman or privy councillor in a district, though there were some exceptions. According to his commission, he was to put his district into the best possible state of defence, to which end he was authorized to muster everyone eligible for service overseas or in the trained bands, arm them, drill them, and if necessary discipline them by invoking martial law. If martial law were needed, a provost marshal was to be appointed to execute it. Lastly, all other local officials were to obey and assist lieutenants and their deputies.

Throughout, the Crown's policy was *ad hoc* and reflected military and political needs. But the appointments assisted stability for two reasons. First, lieutenants were given direct lines of communication to the Privy Council; second, the function matched military needs to aristocratic traditions. The defence of the realm against the Crown's enemies was the ancient role of the nobility, satisfying their honour and justifying their privileges. Yet whereas under Henry VII's and Henry VIII's military system the nobility mustered their feudal retinues as quasi-independent territorial magnates, Elizabeth's lieutenants were agents of the Crown who could be dismissed or summoned to answer for their conduct. And since so many were privy councillors, they responded more readily to central government initiatives than did JPs. They sent a steady flow of information from the localities back to the Privy Council, forging a bilateral chain of communication between central and local government. The tempo visibly quickened in local administration as better records were kept, ordnance depots were established, new transport facilities were provided, members of the trained bands began to be recruited for overseas service alongside the forced levies, and elaborate arrangements were made for one county to send its men to defend another.

Yet the strain of a war economy was cumulative: 105,800

men were impressed for service in the Netherlands, France, Portugal, and Ireland during the last eighteen years of the reign. Conscription for Ireland after 1595 aroused the greatest resentment. In 1600 there was a near mutiny of Kentish cavalry at Chester as they travelled to Ulster. So pressure on the counties led to administrative breakdowns and opposition to central government's demands, while disruption of trade, outbreaks of plague (much of it imported by soldiers returning from abroad), ruined harvests in 1596 and 1597, and acute economic depression caused widespread resentment. Yet the idea of an Elizabethan 'slide to disaster' remains unproven. In the 1590s tension between 'Court' and 'country' was neither as ideological as it was under Charles I, nor did it represent much more than war-weariness and dislike of fiscal burdens. Even in 1598–1601, local resistance to official demands remained largely passive, with exceptions only in coastal counties such as Norfolk.

At the level of central government, however, rising corruption signalled the drift towards venality. In particular, the shortage of Crown patronage during the long war and log-jam in promotion prospects encouraged a traffic in offices. Corruption was not inevitable: official salaries had been raised by Henry VIII, while improved methods of provisioning and the possibility of taking subsistence allowances in either cash or kind compensated to an extent for the rising cost of living. So corruption sprang less from poverty than from increased tolerance of dishonesty during the 1590s. On the other hand, the patronage log-jam was genuine. Whereas the Crown possessed 1,200 or so offices worthy of a gentleman's standing in Elizabeth's reign, Henry VIII had enjoyed similar patronage at a time when aspiring gentry were fewer and official pluralism less pronounced. Also the Reformation had ended the system whereby many of the Crown's bureaucrats were rewarded by preferment as non-resident clergy. Yet research suggests that Elizabeth staved off the worst abuses of the patronage system during her reign. She vetted candidates for office, while contriving to ensure that her discretion was not undermined by collusion between suitors and courtiers. If she suspected deceit, she would invoke her talent for procrastination. Competition at Court, especially during the war years, nevertheless created a 'black market' in which influence was bought and sold. Offices were overtly traded, but unlike Henry VII's sales, the Crown rarely profited financially. Payments were made instead to courtiers to influence the queen's choice: benefit to the Crown was restricted to the increase in New Year's gifts Elizabeth received when appointments were pending. So for a minor post £200 or so would be offered, with competitive bids of £1,000 to £4,000 taken for such lucrative offices as the receivership of the court of wards or treasurership at war. And bids were investments, since if an appointment resulted, the new incumbent would so exercise his office as to recoup his outlay plus interest, for which reason the system was corrupt by Tudor as well as modern standards because the public interest was sacrificed to private gain.

Where late Elizabethan government aroused more vocal dissent was in the matters of licences and monopolies. Clashes in 1597 and 1601 were the ugliest in Parliament during the Tudor period. They signalled unequivocal resentment of abuses promoted by courtiers and government officials. True, some monopolies or licences were genuine patents or copyrights, while others established trading companies with overseas bases which also provided valuable consular services for merchants abroad. But many were designed simply to corner the market in commodities for the patentees, or to grant them exclusive rights which enabled them to demand payments from manufacturers or tradesmen for carrying out their legitimate businesses. They had doubled the price of steel; tripled that of starch; caused that of imported glasses to rise fourfold; and that of salt elevenfold. Courtiers enforced them with impunity, since patents rested on royal prerogative—the common-law courts lacked the power to vet them without royal assent. Indignation was first vented in Parliament in the 1570s, but it was the late Elizabethan mushrooming of monopolies that provoked the backlash. When the young lawyer, William Hakewill, cried, 'Is not bread there?', Elizabeth had personally to intervene to neutralize the attack. And in 1601 she averted the crisis at the expense of the patentees: a proclamation annulled twelve monopolies condemned in Parliament and authorized subjects grieved by other patents to seek redress in the courts of common law.

The final criticism levelled against late Elizabethan government is that the benefits of the Poor Laws were crushed by the rise of Tudor population and economic distress of the 1590s. Although this question raises problems, a Malthusian diagnosis can be eliminated. The Elizabethan state profited from a steadily rising birth-rate that coincided with increased life expectancy. In particular, mortality emergencies of 1586–7 and 1594–8 were not national in geographical extent. The death-rate jumped by 21 per cent in 1596–7, and by a further 5 per cent in 1597–8. But fewer parishes experienced crisis mortality than during the influenza epidemic of 1555–9. And later economic depressions in 1625–6 and 1638–9 were more severe. On the other hand, agricultural prices climbed higher in real terms in 1594–8 than at any time before 1615, while real wages plunged lower in 1597 than at any time between 1260 and 1950. Perhaps two-fifths of the population fell below the margin of subsistence: malnutrition reached the point of starvation in the uplands of Cumbria; disease spread unchecked; reported crimes against property increased; and thousands of families were thrown on to parish relief.

So in a material sense the Poor Laws must have been inadequate. The estimated cash yield of endowed charities for poor relief by 1600 totalled £11,700 per annum—one-quarter of one per cent of national income. Yet the estimated amount raised by poor rates was smaller. If these figures are correct, what was audible was not a bang but a whimper. Yet food and enclosure riots were markedly fewer than might be expected. At a different level the Poor Laws operated as a placebo: the 'labouring poor' were persuaded that their social superiors shared their view of the social order and denounced the same 'caterpillars of the commonwealth'—chiefly middlemen.

The pessimism of the Tudor twilight is partially balanced by positive advances, notably in domestic housing. The years from 1570 to 1610 have no formal significance, but they nevertheless mark the first key phase of the English housing revolution. Probate inventories suggest that from 1530 to 1569 the average size of the Tudor house was three rooms. Between 1570 and the end of Elizabeth's reign it was four or five rooms. The period 1610–42, which was the second phase of the revolution, saw the figure rise to six or more rooms. After 1570, prosperous yeomen might have six, seven, or eight rooms; husbandmen might aspire to two or three rooms, as opposed to the one-room cottages ubiquitous in 1500. Richer farmers would build a chamber over the open hall, replacing the open hearth with a chimney stack. Poorer people favoured ground-floor extensions: a kitchen, or second bedchamber, would be added to an existing cottage. Kitchens were often separate buildings, probably to reduce the risk of fire. A typical late Elizabethan farmstead might be described as 'one dwelling house of three bays, one barn of three bays, one kitchen of one bay'. Meanwhile there were corresponding improvements in domestic comfort. The average investment in hard and soft furniture, tableware, and kitchenware in Tudor England prior to 1570 was around £7. Between 1570 and 1603 it rose to £10. 10s., and in the early Stuart period it climbed to £17. The value of household goods of wealthier families rose by 250 per cent between 1570 and 1610, and that of middling and lesser persons slightly exceeded even that high figure. These percentages were in excess of the inflation rate.

In the upper echelons of society, Elizabethan great houses were characterized by innovations founded on Tudor stability and rising standards of comfort. English architecture after about 1580 was inspired by Gothic ideals of chivalry as much as by Renaissance classicism. The acres of glass and towering symmetry of Hardwick Hall, Derbyshire, built in 1591–7 by Robert Smythson for Elizabeth, countess of Shrewsbury, paid homage to the Perpendicular splendour of King's College Chapel, Cambridge. But if Elizabethan Gothic architecture was neo-medieval in its outward profile, the aim was for enhanced standards of sophistication within. In any case, the neo-medieval courtyards, gatehouses, moats, parapets, towers, and turrets of Tudor England were ornamental, not utilitarian. The parapets at Hardwick incorporated the initials E.S. (Elizabeth Shrewsbury)—the decorative device that proclaimed the parvenue. Brick chimneys became a familiar feature of Tudor mansions, and they signified the arrival of the kitchen and service quarters within the main house, either into a wing or a semi-basement. As time progressed, basement services became fairly common, and were particularly favoured in town houses built on restricted sites. Household servants began to be relegated to the subterranean caverns from which it took three centuries to rescue them.

Yet this was not coincidental. The Elizabethan mansion was the first of its genre to equate privacy with domestic comfort. The great hall of the medieval manor house was not abandoned, but it gave way to the long gallery, hung with historical portraits, where private conversations could be conducted without constant interruption from the traffic of servants. In fact, these Elizabethan long galleries were modelled on those erected in Tudor palaces earlier in the century. An interesting early example was Wolsey's gallery at Hampton Court, where in 1527 Henry VIII and Sir Thomas More had paced uneasily together as they first discussed the terms of the king's proposed divorce. In similar fashion, ground-floor parlours replaced the great hall as the customary family sitting and dining-rooms—at least for normal daily purposes. The family lived in the ground-floor parlours and the first-floor chambers; the servants worked on both these floors and in the basement, and slept in the attics or turrets. Staircases were revitalized as a result: the timber-framed structure gradually became an architectural feature in itself. Finally, provision of fresh-water supplies and improved sanitary arrangements reflected the Renaissance concern with private and public health. In the case of town houses, the family would often go to immense lengths to solve drainage problems, sometimes paying a cash composition to the municipal authorities, but frequently performing some service for the town at Court or at Westminster in return for unlimited water or drainage.

These improvements in Tudor housing were complemented by technical progress in the fields of art and music. Nicholas Hilliard became the most influential painter at the Elizabethan Court on the strength of his ravishing miniatures. Trained as a goldsmith, Hilliard earned renown for his techniques as a 'limner', or illuminator of portrait gems that captured the 'lovely graces, witty smilings, and these stolen glances which suddenly like lightning pass, and another countenance taketh place.' Intimacy was the key to this style, combined with a wealth of emblematic allusion that added intellectual depth to the mirror-like image portrayals. In Hilliard's hands, the miniature was far more than a mere reduced version of an easel painting—but that was thanks to his creative invention. To enhance the techniques learned in the workshops of Ghent and Bruges, where the miniature was painted on fine vellum and pasted on to card, Hilliard used gold as a metal, burnishing it 'with a pretty little tooth of some ferret or stoat or other wild little beast'. Diamond effects were simulated with utter conviction, and Hilliard's jewel-bedecked lockets were often worn as talismans, or exchanged as pledges of love between sovereign and subject or knight and lady. Hilliard's techniques were passed on to his pupil, Isaac Oliver, and finally to Samuel Cooper. The miniature was ultimately confounded by the invention of photography.

Tudor music was invigorated by royal and noble patronage, by the continued liturgical demands of the Church, and by the steady abandonment of the strict modal limitations of the medieval period in favour of more progressive techniques of composition and performance. The Tudor monarchs, together with Cardinal Wolsey, were distinguished patrons of music both sacred and secular. An inventory of Henry VIII's musical instruments suggests that as lavish a selection was available in

England as anywhere in Europe—the king himself favoured the lute and organ. His and Wolsey's private chapels competed to recruit the best organists and singers to be found in England and Wales. In Mary's reign, England was exposed to the potent artistry of Flemish and Spanish music, while the seminal influence of Italy was always present in the shape of Palestrina's motets and the works of the Florentine madrigalists. Elizabeth I retained a large corps of Court musicians drawn from Italy, Germany, France, and England itself. But her Chapel Royal was the premier conservatoire of Tudor musical talent and invention, for Thomas Tallis, William Byrd, and John Bull made their careers there. The Protestant Reformation happily encouraged, rather than abandoned, composers—the Edwardian and Elizabethan injunctions left liturgical music intact, and many of the gentlemen of the Chapel discreetly remained Catholics, including Byrd and Bull. Yet it was the technical advances that really mattered. Byrd and Bull gradually freed themselves from the old ecclesiastical modes, or ancient scales. Tallis and Byrd gained a licence for music printing that enabled them to pioneer printed musical notation, albeit unsuccessfully. Melody, harmony, and rhythm became as important to music as plainsong and counterpoint, and the arts of ornamentation and extemporization thrived among the virginalists, and among the lute and consort players. Such developments presaged the music of seventeenth-century English and Continental composers, and ultimately that of J. S. Bach.

The age of the Tudors ended on an equivocal note, which is best discerned in its literature. Erasmus's wit and More's satirical fiction expressed (though in Latin) the intellectual exuberance of pre-Reformation Europe. Sir Thomas Elyot, Sir John Cheke, and Roger Ascham translated Renaissance ideals into pedestrian but tolerable English prose. Sir Thomas Wyatt, Henry Howard, earl of Surrey, and Sir Philip Sidney reanimated English lyric poetry and rekindled the sonnet as the vehicle of eloquent and classical creativity. But it was Edmund Spenser who rediscovered to perfection what English prosody had lacked since the time of Chaucer. Once again, music tutored the ear, and the connections between ear and tongue were fully realized. Spenser attained an impeccable mastery of rhythm, time, and tune—his work was no mere 'imitation of the ancients'. In particular, his harmonious blend of northern and midland with southern dialects permitted verbal modulations and changes of diction and mood akin to those of lute players. His pastoral sequence, *The Shepheards Calendar* (1579), was a landmark in the history of English poetry, its melodious strains encapsulating the pains and pleasures of pastoral life.

> Colin, to heare thy rymes and roundelayes,
> Which thou wert wont on wastfull hylls to singe,
> I more delight then larke in Sommer dayes;
> Whose Echo made the neyghbour groves to ring,
> And taught the byrds, which in the lower spring
> Did shroude in shady leaves from sonny rayes,
> Frame to thy songe their chereful cheriping,
> Or hold theyr peace, for shame of thy swete layes.

Spenser's masterpiece was *The Faerie Queene* (1589 and 1596), an allegorical epic poem, which examined on a dazzling multiplicity of levels the nature and quality of the late-Elizabethan polity. The form of the poem was Gothic as much as Renaissance: the Gothic 'revival' in architecture after 1580 was paralleled by its episodic sequences, within which details took on their own importance, decorating the external symmetry without damaging the total effect. The poem above all, though, was an allegory. As Spenser explained in a dedicatory epistle to Sir Walter Raleigh, 'In that Fairy Queen I mean glory in my general intention, but in my particular I conceive the most excellent and glorious person of our sovereign the Queen, and her kingdom in Fairy land. And yet, in some places else, I do otherwise shadow her.' In other words, Spenser's allegory was part moral, part fictional—there was no easy or straightforward correspondence of meaning. Yet the allegory had a single end; as in *Piers Plowman* before it, and *Pilgrim's Progress* afterwards, *The Faerie Queene* led the reader along the path upon which truth was distinguishable from falsehood. To this end, the ambition, corruption, intrigue, and secular-mindedness of Elizabethan power politics were sublimated into the 'delightful land of Faerie', clothed in the idyllic garments of romance, and exalted as the fictional realization of the golden age of Gloriana.

It was inevitable that Spenser should fail to impress the Elizabethan establishment. He informed Raleigh that his 'general end' was 'to fashion a gentleman or noble person in virtuous and gentle discipline'. Yet the ambiguities were pervasive: Spenser saw his goal as already archaic. Chivalry had been soured by Renaissance politics and statecraft; the 'verray parfit, gentil knyght' of Chaucer's age had been displaced by the Tudor courtier. The golden age had passed, if it had ever existed:

> So oft as I with state of present time
> The image of the antique world compare,
> When as mans age was in his freshest prime,
> And the first blossome of faire vertue bare;
> Such oddes I finde twixt those, and these which are,
> As that, through long continuance of his course,
> Me seemes the world is runne quite out of square
> From the first point of his appointed sourse;
> And being once amisse growes daily wourse and wourse.

Spenser's allegory in *The Faerie Queene* was unquestionably over-complex; his attempt to fuse worldly and idealized principles of behaviour into a single dramatic epic was bound to prove unmanageable. Moreover, the reader was obliged to unriddle endless personifications of Elizabeth as the moon-goddess Diana (or Cynthia or Belphoebe), of Sir Walter Raleigh as Timias, of Mary Stuart as Duessa, who also doubled as Theological Falsehood—and so on. However, Spenser's failure to convince, as opposed to his poetic ability to delight, actually *heightens* our impression of his disillusion and despair. We are taught to debunk the myth of Gloriana; art has held 'the mirror up to nature' and shown 'the very age and body of the time his form and pressure'.

Another faithful mirror of the Tudor age was that held by the immortal William Shakespeare. Author of thirty-eight plays that included *Hamlet* (1600–1), *King Lear* (1605–6), and *Othello* (1604), and of 154 Sonnets (1593–7), together with *Venus and Adonis* and *The Rape of Lucrece* (1593–4), Shakespeare has exerted greater influence on English literature and European drama than any other single writer. The sheer vitality, power, and virtuosity of his work remain unmatched in any European language; his genius exceeded that of Chaucer or Tennyson—it need not be justified or explained. We should, however, remember that Shakespeare was not an 'intellectual' or 'élitist' writer, like Milton or Voltaire. His orbit centred on Stratford and London, not Oxford and Cambridge. His was the everyday world of life, death, money, passion, stage business, and the alehouse—such matters became the stuff of peerless drama and poetry. The rich variety of his experience is perhaps the chief reason for the universality of his appeal; certainly there is no hint of the bigot or intellectual snob in his work.

Shakespeare's experience was, nevertheless, that of a writer at the cultural crossroads of Europe. After about 1580, European literature explored increasingly the modes of individual expression and characterization associated with modern processes of thought. Authors and the fictional characters they created displayed awareness both of experience in general, and of themselves as the particular agents of unique experiences. Shakespeare's *Hamlet* and Christopher Marlowe's *Doctor Faustus* (1592) epitomize the dramatic depiction of individual experience in Elizabethan literature. Of the two plays, *Hamlet* is the more advanced. Shakespeare took a familiar plot and transformed it into a timeless masterpiece. But Marlowe's *Faustus* was not far behind. Both dramatists were eager to pursue psychology, rather than ethics. The difference is that Faustus does not pass beyond the bounds of egotism and self-dramatization to realize self-analysis, whereas Hamlet's subjective introspection and self-doubts are the keystones of the action.

What a piece of work is a man! how noble in reason! how infinite in faculties! in form and moving, how express and admirable! in action, how like an angel! in apprehension, how like a god! the beauty of the world! the paragon of animals! And yet to me, what is this quintessence of dust?

(Hamlet, II. ii. 323–9)

Neoplatonist philosophy as practised at the dawn of the sixteenth century by John Colet and his circle had dealt with the objective appreciation of senses, natures, and truth—this reflected the medieval cast of mind. Eighty or so years later, the emphasis had shifted towards subjectivity and self-expression, paradoxically under the influence of Calvinist theology, which so stressed the inflexibility of God's predestined Word that a person's quest for grace necessarily came to depend on systematic self-scrutiny. Calvinism was also replacing the medieval ideal of chivalry with the notion of the permanent spiritual warfare of God's elect against worldly thraldom.

Marlowe and Shakespeare dominated Elizabethan drama, although they did not monopolize it. The allegories and morality plays of the fifteenth century flourished until suppressed, especially in such provincial towns as Chester, Coventry, and York. But the Brave New World was symbolized by Shakespeare's Globe Theatre in London, where the impact of the Protestant Reformation had combined with the enhanced sophistication of metropolitan life to give distinctive shape to the preferred drama of modern Britain. Self-expression, individuality, and the soliloquy were the cultural developments that paralleled the expansion of education and literacy, the birth of the nonconformist conscience, and the growth of cosmopolitan attitudes.

Yet Hamlet's melancholy defeated his self-knowledge. He remained uncertain of his destiny, and of the reason for his existence:

> To be, or not to be: that is the question:
> Whether 'tis nobler in the mind to suffer

> The slings and arrows of outrageous fortune,
> Or to take arms against a sea of troubles,
> And by opposing end them? To die: to sleep;
> No more; and, by a sleep to say we end
> The heart-ache and the thousand natural shocks
> That flesh is heir to, 'tis a consummation
> Devoutly to be wish'd.
>
> (*Hamlet*, III. i. 56–64)

Such sentiments were equally applicable to the dusk of Tudor England. When the bell tolled for the age of Gloriana, on 24 March 1603, Elizabeth had already lost her will to survive, Burghley was five years dead, and a newly ambitious and less scrupulous generation of courtiers was ascendant. It is easy to romanticize or eulogize such Tudor triumphs as stability, economic expansion, the Reformation, the repulse of Spain, the defeat of Protestant and Catholic extremism, and the unification of Britain—finally attained on Elizabeth's death. But reality is more abrasive. Stability had begun to breed instability through structural decay. By the 1620s England would be unable to fight a protracted war without engendering domestic political friction. When Clarendon later began his *History of the Rebellion and Civil Wars* he wrote: 'I am not so sharp-sighted as those, who have discerned this rebellion contriving from (if not before) the death of Queen Elizabeth.' He knew that if we read history backwards, Elizabeth's inertia and immobility in the 1590s, combined with the rise of 'venality' at Court, could be said to have established a pattern that precluded comprehensive reform. But history is properly read forwards. When this is done, it is clear that a 'slide to disaster' was unlikely in the sixteenth century. Elizabeth controlled her own policy; the Privy Council was a tightly organized body; communications with the localities were good; a Protestant consensus had emerged. Yet the Tudor legacy of meagre public revenue and endemic corruption in the central bureaucracy was ultimately ameliorated *by* the events of the Civil War and Interregnum.

2. The Stuarts
(1603–1688)

JOHN MORRILL

THE Stuarts were one of England's least successful dynasties. Charles I was put on public trial for treason and was publicly beheaded; James II fled the country fearing a similar fate, and abandoned his kingdom and throne. James I and Charles II died peacefully in their beds, but James I lived to see all his hopes fade and ambitions thwarted, while Charles II, although he had the trappings of success, was a curiously unambitious man, whose desire for a quiet life was not achieved until it was too late for him to enjoy it. Towering above the Stuart age were the two decades of civil war, revolution, and republican experiment which ought to have changed fundamentally the course of English history, but which did so, if at all, very elusively. Whilst kings and generals toiled and failed, however, a fundamental change was taking place in English economy and society, largely unheeded and certainly unfashioned by the will of government. In fact, the most obvious revolution in seventeenth-century England was the consequence of a decline in the birth-rate.

Society and Economic Life

The population of England had been growing steadily from the early sixteenth century, if not earlier. It continued to grow in the first half of the seventeenth century. The total population of England in 1600 was probably fairly close to 4.1 million (and Scotland, Ireland, and Wales, much more impressionistically, 1.9 million). By the mid-century, the population of England had reached a peak of almost 5.3 million, and the total for Britain had risen from roughly 6.0 to roughly 7.7 million. Thereafter, the number stabilized, or may even have sagged to 4.9 million in England, 7.3 million in Britain. The reasons for the rise in population, basically a steady progression with occasional setbacks resulting from epidemics before 1650, and the subsequent relapse, are very puzzling. The best recent research has placed most emphasis on the family-planning habits of the population. Once the plague had lost its virulence, a country like England, in which land was plentiful and extremes of weather never such as to wipe out entire harvests, was likely to see population growth. Each marriage was likely to produce more than enough children who would survive to adulthood to maintain the population. The rate of population growth was in fact kept rather low by the English custom of late marriage. In all social groups, marriage was usually deferred until both partners were in their mid-twenties and the wife had only twelve to fifteen childbearing years before her. The reason for this pattern of late marriage seems to be the firm convention that the couple save up enough money to launch themselves as an independent household before they wed. For the better off, this frequently meant university, legal training, an apprenticeship of seven years or more; for the less well off a long term of domestic service, living in with all found but little in the way of cash wages.

This pattern continued into the late seventeenth century with even later marriages; perhaps the real earnings of the young had fallen so that sufficient savings took longer to generate. At any rate the average age of first marriage seems to have risen by a further two years to over twenty-six, with a consequent effect on fertility. More dramatic still is the evidence of a will to restrict family size. Steps were clearly taken in families with three or more children to prevent or inhibit further conceptions. For example, mothers would breast-feed third or subsequent children for many more months than they would their first or second child, with the (effective) intention of lowering fertility. Crude contraceptive devices and sexual prudence were also clearly widespread. Some studies of gentry families even suggest that celibacy became much more common (the growth of the Navy may be partly responsible for this unexpected development!). In South Wales, one in three of all heads of leading gentry families remained unmarried in the late seventeenth century compared with a negligible proportion one hundred years earlier; while the average numbers of children per marriage declined from five to two and a half (which, given the high rate of child mortality, meant that a high proportion of those families died out). It is not known whether this was typical of the gentry everywhere or of other social groups. But it does graphically illustrate changing demographic patterns.

The economic, social, and political consequences were momentous. In the century before 1640, population was growing faster than food resources. One result of this was occasional and localized food shortages so severe as to occasion hunger, starvation, and death. It is possible that some Londoners died of starvation at the end of the sixteenth and at the beginning of the seventeenth-centuries and quite certain that many did so in Cumbria in the early 1620s. Thereafter, famine disappears as a visible threat, in England at least. Increased agricultural production, better communication and lines of credit, and the levelling off of population solved the problem. England escaped the periodic dearths and widespread starvation that were to continue to devastate its continental neighbours for decades to come.

A more persistent effect of population growth was price inflation. Food prices rose eightfold in the period 1500–1640, wages less than threefold. For most of those who did not produce their own food, and enough of it to feed themselves and their household with a surplus to sell in the market, it was a century of financial attrition. Above all, for the growing proportion of the nation who depended upon wage-labouring, the century witnessed a major decline in living standards. In fact, a large section of the population—certainly a majority—had to buy much of their food, and these purchases took up an increasing proportion of their income. It became a central concern of government to regulate the grain trade and to provide both local machinery and an administrative code, backed up by legal sanctions, to ensure that whenever there was harvest failure, available stocks of grain and other produce were made widely available at the lowest extra cost which could be achieved.

A growing population put pressure not only on food resources but on land. With families producing on average more than one son, either family property had to be divided, reducing the endowment of each member for the next generation, or one son took over the family land or tenancy while the others had to fend for themselves. The high prices of agricultural produce made it worth while to plough, or otherwise to farm marginal lands hitherto uneconomic, but in most regions by the early seventeenth century there was little unoccupied land left to be so utilized. The way forward lay with the more productive use of existing farmed land, particularly in woodland areas or in the Fenland where existing conditions (inundations by the sea or winter rain) made for only limited usage. The problem here was that the drainage of the Fens or the clearing of woodland areas was costly, had to be undertaken by those with risk capital, and had to be at the expense of the life-style, livelihood, and modest prosperity of those who lived there. Once again, government was forced to be active in mediating (or more often vacillating) between encouraging higher productivity and guarding against the anguish and protest of those adversely affected.

A growing population also put pressure on jobs. By the early seventeenth century there was widespread underemployment in England. Agriculture remained the major source of employment, but the work in the fields was seasonal and hundreds of thousands found lay labouring sufficient for part but not all of the year. Because, however, labour was plentiful and cheap, because most manufacturing relied exclusively on muscle power rather than a form of energy that would draw workers to its source, because raw materials walked about on, grew up out of, or lay dormant within the land, 'industry' in the seventeenth century took place in cottages and outbuildings of rural village communities. For some, especially in the metal-working and building trades, 'manufacturing' would be the primary source of income. For others, as in some textile trades, it could be a primary or secondary source of income. Textiles were by far the largest 'manufacture' with perhaps 200,000 workers scattered throughout England, above all in the south-west, in East Anglia, or in the Pennine region. It was a particularly volatile industry, however, with high food prices dampening the domestic market and war and foreign competition sharply reducing foreign markets in the early seventeenth century. Tens of thousands of families, however, could not balance the household budget whatever they tried. Injury, disability, or death made them particularly vulnerable to a short-fall of revenue. There was chronic 'under-employment': a structural problem of too many part-time workers seeking full-time work.

At Aldenham in Hertfordshire, about one in ten households needed regular support from the poor rate but a further one in four (making over one-third in all) needed occasional doles or allowances (for example of fuel or clothes) to ease them through difficult patches. For a large number of families, achieving subsistence involved scrounging or scavenging fuel or wild fruit and vegetables and seeking periodic help from local charities or the rates—what has been called the 'economy of makeshifts'. One effect of the difficulties of rural employment was to drive large numbers of men and women into the cities—above all to London—where the problems were no less but rather more volatile. There was a large amount of casual unskilled labour in the towns, but casual work could shrink rapidly in times of recession or harvest failure. High food prices meant less demand for other goods and this in turn meant less scope for non-agricultural wages. Those who most needed additional wages for food were most likely to find less work available. Once more, the government had been drawn in to organize and superintend a national scheme of poor relief, and ancillary codes of practice governing geographical mobility, house building, and the promotion of overseas trade. Thus a growing population greatly increased the duties and responsib-ilities of the government, arguably beyond the Crown's re-sources and capacity. Those who produced and sold goods, those who could benefit from the land hunger in increased rents and dues, and those who serviced an increasingly complex and uncertain market in lands and goods (notably the lawyers) wanted to enjoy the fruits of their success; others looked to the Crown to prevent or to mitigate the effects of structural change. A dynamic economy is one in which government has to arbitrate between competing and irreconcilable interests. No wonder the Crown found itself disparaged and increasingly distrusted.

By contrast, the late seventeenth-century saw the easing, if not the disappearance, of these problems. The slight population decline in itself prevented the problems from getting worse. The upsurge in agricultural productivity was more important. The nature and extent of agricultural change in the seventeenth century is still much disputed. What is clear is that England ceased from about the 1670s to be a net importer of grain and became an exporter; indeed, bounties had to be introduced to ensure that surplus stocks were not hoarded. This remarkable turn-around may have been the result of a massive extension of the acreage under the plough—either by the ploughing of land not hitherto farmed or by land amelioration schemes. But it might also be the result of the introduction of new methods of farming which dramatically increased the yield per acre. By skilful alternation of crops and more extensive use of manure and fertilizers, it is possible to increase yields of grain and to sustain much greater livestock levels. Almost all the ideas which were to transform English agriculture down to the early nineteenth century were known about by 1660; indeed most of them had been tried and tested in the Netherlands. The problem is to discover how rapidly they were taken up. There was stubborn conservatism, especially among the yeomen; the good ideas lay mingled in the textbooks with some equally plausible ones which were in fact specious; the most effective methods required considerable rationalization of land use and some of them required high capital outlay. In the early part of the century, it seems likely that the most widespread innovations were not those which increased yields, but those which soaked up cheap surplus employment—especially 'industrial' cash crops that had to be turned into manufactures: dye crops, tobacco, mulberry trees (for silkworms). It was only when a falling population raised real wages and lowered grain prices that the impetus to increase productivity replaced the desire to extend the scale of operation as a primary motivation of the farmer. Changes in the way land was rented out also gave the landlord better prospects of seeing a return on the money he invested in land leased out. The new farming probably consolidated the position established earlier by the simple device of increasing the acreage under the plough. Either way, government action in the grain market and the regulation of wages became far less frequent and necessary.

In 1600, England still consisted of a series of regional economies striving after, if not always achieving, self-sufficiency. Problems of credit and of distribution hindered the easy exchange of produce between regions. Most market towns, even the large county towns, were principally places where the produce of the area was displayed and sold. By 1690 this was no longer the case. England had for long been the largest free trade area in Europe and had the Crown had its way at most points in the century, the full integration of Ireland and Scotland into a customs-free zone would have been achieved or brought nearer. That it was not owed most to the narrow self-interest of lobbyists in the House of Commons, especially in the 1600s and the 1660s. No point in England was (or is) more than seventy-five miles from the sea, and as a result of the schemes to improve river navigation, few places by 1690 were more than twenty miles from water navigable to the sea. Gradually, a single, integrated national economy was emerging. No longer did each region have to strive for self-sufficiency, producing low-quality goods in poor-grade soil or inhospitable climate. Regional specializations could emerge, taking full advantage of soil and climatic conditions, which could then be exchanged for surplus grain or dairy products from elsewhere. Hence, the spread of market-gardening in Kent.

Exactly the same could be said for manufactures. One consequence of and further stimulus to this was a retailing revolution—the coming of age of the shop. The characteristic of market towns was the market-stall or shambles, in which the stall-holders or retailers displayed their own wares which they had grown, made, or at least finished from local raw materials. By 1690, most towns, even quite small ones, had shops in the modern sense: places which did not distribute the produce of the region but which met the variegated needs of the region. The shopkeeper met those needs from far and wide. One particularly well-documented example is William Stout who, in the 1680s, rented a shop in Lancaster for £5 per annum. He visited London and Sheffield and bought goods worth over £200, paid for half in cash (a legacy from his father), half on credit. Soon he was purchasing goods from far and wide and offering the people of Lancaster and its environs a wide variety of produce: West Indian sugar, American tobacco, West Riding iron-mongery, and so on. None the less, once towns became centres for the distribution of the produce of the world, people would tend to bypass the smaller towns with little choice and make for the bigger centres with maximum choice. This is why most seventeenth-century urban growth was concentrated in existing large market towns. The proportion of the population living in the twenty or so towns which already had 10,000 inhabitants rose sharply; the proportion living in the smaller market towns actually fell slightly. Some small centres of manufacturing (metalworking towns such as Birmingham and Sheffield, or cloth-finishing towns such as Manchester or Leeds, or ship-building towns such as Chatham) became notable urban centres. But the twenty largest towns in 1690 were almost the same as the twenty largest in 1600. All of them were on the coast or on navigable rivers.

Large towns, then, prospered because of their changing role in marketing. But many of them—and county towns especially—increasingly concentrated not only on the sale of goods; they began to concentrate on the sale of services. The pull of the shops and the burgeoning importance of county towns as local administrative centres in which hundreds gathered regularly for local courts and commissions, encouraged the service and leisure industries. Gentlemen and prosperous farmers came to town for business or for the shops, and would stop to take professional advice from lawyers, doctors, estate agents; or bring their families and stay over for a round of social exchanges linked by visits to the theatre, concerts, or new recreational facilities. The age of the spa and the resort was dawning.

Paris, the largest town in France, had 350,000 inhabitants in the mid-seventeenth century. The second and third largest were Rouen and Lyons with 80,000–100,000 inhabitants. In Europe, there were only five towns with populations of more than 250,000, but over one hundred with more than 50,000 inhabitants. In England, however, London had well over half a million inhabitants by 1640 or 1660; Newcastle, Bristol, and Norwich, which rivalled one another for second place, had barely 25,000 each. London was bigger than the next fifty towns in England combined. It is hard to escape the conclusion that London was growing at the expense of the rest. Its stranglehold on overseas trade, and therefore on most of the early banking and financial activity, was slow to ease; in consequence much of the trade from most of the outports had to be directed via London. In the seventeenth century the major new 're-export' trades (the importation of colonial raw materials such as sugar and tobacco for finishing and dispatch to Europe) were concentrated there. London dominated the governmental, legal, and political world. While rural England flourished under the opportunities to feed the capital and keep its inhabitants warm, urban growth was probably slowed. By 1640, 10 per cent of all Englishmen lived in the capital, and one in six had lived part of their lives there. By 1690 the richest one hundred Londoners were among the richest men in England. No longer was wealth primarily the perquisite of the landed.

If goods moved more freely within a national economy, people may have become more rooted in their own community. Both before and after the Civil War, more than two-thirds of all Englishmen died in a parish different from the one in which they were born. But both before and after the wars, most did not move far; most stayed within their county of birth. It is possible to distinguish two patterns of migration. The first is 'betterment migration' as adolescents and young adults moved to take up apprenticeship or tenancies of farms. This migration throughout the century was essentially local except for movement from all over the country to London for apprenticeships. The second is 'subsistence migration', as those who found no work or prospect of work at home took to the road, often travelling long distances in the hope of finding employment elsewhere. Such migration was far more common in the first half of the century than in the second, partly because demographic stagnation and economic development created a better chance of jobs at home, partly because the general easing of demands on poor relief made parish authorities more sympathetic to the able-bodied unemployed, and partly because tough settlement laws inhibited and discouraged migration. An Act of Parliament in 1662 gave constables and overseers power to punish those who moved from parish to parish in search of vacant common land or wasteland on which to build cottages.

The seventeenth century is probably the first in England history in which more people emigrated than immigrated. In the course of the century, something over one-third of a million people—mainly young adult males—emigrated across the Atlantic. The largest single group made for the West Indies; a second substantial group made for Virginia and for Catholic Maryland; a very much smaller group made for Puritan New England. The pattern of emigration was a fluctuating one, but it probably reached its peak in the 1650s and 1660s. For most of those who went, the search for employment and a better life was almost certainly the principal cause of their departure. For a clear minority, however, freedom from religious persecution and the expectation that they could establish churches to worship God in their preferred fashion took precedence. An increasing number were forcibly transported as a punishment for criminal acts or (particularly in the 1650s) simply as a punishment for vagrancy. In addition to the transatlantic settlers, an unknown number crossed the English Channel and settled in Europe. The largest group were probably the sons of Catholic families making for religious houses or mercenary military activity. Younger sons of Protestant gentlemen also enlisted in the latter. Many hundreds were to return to fight the English Civil War. Thus, whereas the sixteenth century had seen England become a noted haven for religious refugees, in the seventeenth century Europe and America received religious refugees from England. The early seventeenth century probably saw less immigration from abroad than for many decades before. The only significant immigration in the seventeenth century was of Jews who flocked in after the Cromwellian regime had removed the legal bars on their residence, and of French Huguenots escaping from Louis XIV's persecution in the 1680s.

Fewer men set up home far from the place of their birth. But many more men travelled the length and breadth of England. There was a tripling or a quadrupling of the number of packmen, carriers, and others engaged in moving goods about. The tunnage of shipping engaged in coastal trading probably rose by the same amount. The roads were thronged with petty chapmen, with their news-sheets, tracts, almanacs, cautionary tales, pamphlets full of homespun wisdom; pedlars with trinkets of all sorts; and travelling entertainers. If the alehouse had always been a distraction from that other social centre of village life, the parish church, it now became much more its rival in the dissemination of news and information and in the formation of popular culture. In the early years of the century, national and local regulation of alehouses was primarily concerned with ensuring that not too much of the barley harvest was malted and brewed; by the end of the century, regulation was more concerned with the pub's potential for sedition.

In the century from 1540 to 1640 there was a redistribution of wealth away from rich and poor towards those in the middle of society. The richest men in the kingdom derived the bulk of their income from rents and services, and these were notoriously difficult to keep in line with inflation: a tradition of long leases and the custom of fixed rents and fluctuating 'entry fines'—payments made when tenancies changed hands— militated against it. Vigilant landowners could keep pace with inflation, but many were not vigilant. Equally, those whose farms or holdings did not make them self-sufficient suffered rising (and worse, fluctuating) food prices, while a surplus on the labour market and declining real wages made it very hard for the poor to make good the shortfall. The number of landless labourers and cottagers soared. Those in the middle of society, whether yeomen farmers or tradesmen, prospered. If they produced a surplus over and above their own needs they could sell dear and produce more with the help of cheap labour. They could lend their profits to their poorer neighbours (there were after all no banks, stocks and shares, building societies) and foreclose on the debts. They invested in more land, preferring to extend the scale of their operations rather than sink capital into improved productivity. Many of those who prospered from farming rose into the gentry.

Only two groups had 'social' status in seventeenth-century England—the gentry and the peerage. Everybody else had 'economic' status, and was defined by his economic function (husbandman, cobbler, merchant, attorney, etc.). The peerage and gentry were different. They had a 'quality' which set them apart. That 'quality' was 'nobility'. Peers and gentlemen were 'noble'; everybody else was 'ignoble' or 'churlish'. Such concepts were derived partly from the feudal and chivalric traditions in which land was held from the Crown in exchange for the performance of military duties. These duties had long since disappeared, but the notion that the ownership of land and 'manors' conferred status and 'honour' had been reinvigorated by the appropriation to English conditions of Aristotle's notion of the citizen. The gentleman or nobleman was a man set apart to govern. He was independent and leisured: he derived his income without having to work for it, that income made him free from want and from being beholden to or dependent upon others, and he had the time and leisure to devote himself to the arts of government. He was independent in judgement and trained to make decisions. Not all gentlemen served in the offices which required such qualities (justice of the peace, sheriff, militia captain, high constable, etc.). But all had this capacity to serve, to govern. A gentleman was expected to be hospitable, charitable, fair-minded. He was distinguished from his country neighbour, the yeoman, as much by attitude of mind and personal preference as by wealth. Minor gentry and yeomen had similar incomes. But they lived different lives: the gentleman rented out his lands, wore cloth and linen, read Latin; the yeoman was a working farmer, wore leather, read and wrote in English. By 1640, there were perhaps 120 peers and 20,000 gentry, one in twenty of all adult males. The permanence of land and the security of landed income restricted gentility to the countryside; the prosperous merchant or craftsman, though he may have had a larger income than many gentlemen, and have discharged, in the government of his borough, the same duties, was denied the status of gentleman.

He had to work, and his capital and income were insecure. Younger sons of gentlemen, trained up in the law or apprenticed into trade, did not retain their status. But they were put into professions through which they or their sons could redeem it. The wealthy merchant or lawyer had some prospect of buying a manor and settling back into a gentler life-style at the end of his life.

This pattern shifted in the late seventeenth century. Conditions were now against the larger farmer: he had high taxation, higher labour costs, and lower profits, unless he invested heavily in higher productivity, which he was less able to do than the great landowners (for whom there were economies of scale). Few yeomen now aspired to the trappings of gentility, while many minor gentlemen abandoned an unequal struggle to keep up appearances. On the other hand, professional men, merchants, and town governors became bolder in asserting that they were as good as the country gentleman and were entitled to his title of respect. The definition of 'gentility' was stretched to include them without a prior purchase of land. This 'pseudo-gentility' became increasingly respectable and increasingly widely recognized, even by the heralds. It was not, however, recognized by many country gentlemen who bitterly resented this devaluation of their treasured status. They responded to the debasement of the term 'gentry' by sponsoring and promoting a new term which restored their exclusiveness and self-importance: they called themselves squires and their group the 'squirearchy'.

The century between 1540 and 1640 had seen the consolidation of those in the middle of society at the expense of those at the bottom and, to some extent, of those at the top. The century after 1640 saw some relief for the mass of poor householders, increasing difficulties for large farmers and small landowners, rich pickings for those at the top. There was emerging by 1690 (though its great age was just beginning) a group of men whose interests, wealth, and power grew out of, but which extended far beyond, their landed estates. They invested in trade, in government loans, in the mineral resources of their land, as well in improved farming and in renting out farming land. They spent as much time in their town houses as in their country seats; they were as much at home with the wealthy élite in London as with their rural neighbours. They constituted a culturally cosmopolitan élite of transcendent wealth, incorporating many of the peerage, but not confined to them. This new phenomenon was recognized at the time and needed a label, a collective noun. It became known as the aristocracy (a term hitherto a preserve of political thinkers, like democracy, rather than of social analysis). The invention of the term 'squire' and adaptation of the word 'aristocrat' in the late seventeenth century tells us a great deal about the way society was evolving. The integration of town and country, the spread of metropolitan values and fashions, the fluidity of the economy and the mobility of society are all involved in the way men categorized one another. By 1690, England already had a flexible and simple moneyed élite; access to wealth and power was not restricted by outdated notions of privilege and obsessions with purity of birth as in much of Europe.

Government and Law

Stuart governments had little understanding of these structural changes and less ability to influence them. The resources of Stuart government fell far short of those required to carry out the ambitions and expectations which most people had of their king and which kings had of themselves.

The financial and bureaucratic resources at the disposal of kings remained limited. James I inherited an income of £350,000 a year. By the later 1630s this had risen to £1,000,000 a year and by the 1680s to £2,000,000 a year. This is a notable increase. It meant that, throughout the seventeenth century, the Stuarts could finance their activities in peacetime. As the century wore on, revenues from Crown lands and Crown feudal and prerogative right fell away to be an insignificant part of royal revenues. The ordinary revenues of the Crown became predominantly those derived from taxing trade: customs duties on the movement of goods into and out of the country and excise duties, a sales tax on basic consumer goods (above all beer!). Only during the Civil Wars and Interregnum (when a majority of state revenues came from property taxes) did direct taxation play a major part in the budget. Over the period 1603–40 and 1660–89, less than 8 per cent of all royal revenues came from direct taxation—certainly less than in the fourteenth or sixteenth centuries. This, in part, reflects landowner domination of the tax-granting House of Commons; but it also reflects an administrative arthritis that hindered improvements in the efficiency and equity of tax distribution.

The buoyancy of trade, especially after 1630, was the greatest single cause of the steady growth in royal income—well ahead of inflation—that made Stuart monarchy at almost every point the least indebted in Europe. Both James I and Charles II suffered from fiscal incontinence, buying the loyalty and favour of their servants with a rashness that often went beyond what was necessary. However, the problems of the Stuarts can fairly be laid at Elizabeth's door. All over Europe in the sixteenth and seventeenth centuries, princes used the threat of invasion by tyrannical and/or heretical foreigners to create new forms of taxation which were usually made permanent when the invasion scare had receded or was repulsed. William III was to make just such a transformation in the 1690s when England was under siege from the absolutist Louis XIV and the bigoted James II. Since the Stuarts never faced a realistic threat of invasion, they never had a good excuse to insist on unpalatable fiscal innovations. Elizabeth I had a perfect opportunity in the Armada years but she was too old, conservatively advised, too preoccupied even to attempt it. Instead she paid for the war by selling land. Although this did not make James I and Charles I's position as difficult as was once thought, it did have one major consequence: it deprived the king of security against loans.

The Stuarts, then, whenever they put their mind to it, had an

adequate income and a balanced budget. Almost alone amongst
the rulers of the day they never went bankrupt, and only once,
in 1670, had to defer payment of interest on loans. But they
never had enough money to wage successful war. Since,
throughout the century up to 1689, no one ever threatened to
invade England or to declare war on her, this was not as
serious as it sounds. England waged war on Spain (1624–30,
1655–60), on France (1627–30), and on the Netherlands (1651–
4, 1665–7, 1672–4), but always as the aggressor. It cannot be
said that these wars achieved the objectives of those who advocated them, but none was lost in the sense that concessions
were made on the status quo ante. While rivalries in the colonial spheres (South Asia, Africa, North, Central, and South
America) were intensifying, no territories were ceded and expansion continued steadily. There was a growing recognition of
the futility of major armed interventions on the Continent
which led to gradual increases in the proportion of resources
devoted to the navy, while all Continental countries found that
the costs of land warfare hindered the development of their
navies. By 1689 the British navy was the equal of the Dutch and
the French, and the wars of the next twenty-five years were to
make it the dominant navy in Europe. For a country which
could not afford an active foreign policy, England's standing in
the world had improved remarkably during the century.

The monarchy lacked coercive power: there was no standing
army or organized police force. Even the guards regiments
which protected the king and performed ceremonial functions
around him were a Restoration creation. In the period 1603–40
the number of fighting men upon whom the king could call in
an emergency could be counted in scores rather than in
thousands. After 1660 there were probably about 3,000 armed
men on permanent duty in England and rather more in Ireland
and Tangiers (which had come to Charles II as a rather troublesome part of the dowry of his Portuguese wife). There were
then also several thousand Englishmen regimented and in
permanent service with the Dutch and with the Portuguese

armies who could be recalled in emergency. But there was no military presence in England, and apart from pulling up illegal tobacco crops in the west country and occasionally rounding up religious dissidents, the army was not visible until James II's reign.

It had not been so, of course, in the aftermath of the Civil War. At the height of the conflict, in 1643–4, there were probably 150,000 men in arms: one in eight of the adult male population. By the late 1640s, this had fallen to 25,000. The number rose to 45,000 in the third Civil War, waged against the youthful Charles II and the Scots (1650–1), and then fell to remain at between 10,000 and 14,000 for the rest of the decade (although between 18,000 and 40,000 more were serving at any particular moment in Scotland and Ireland). The troops in England were widely dispersed into garrisons. London had a very visible military presence, since 3,000 or so troops were kept in very public places (including St. Paul's Cathedral, the nave of which became a barracks). Everywhere troops could be found meddling in local administration and local politics (and perhaps above all in local churches, for garrisons very often protected and nurtured radical, separatist meeting-houses). The army was at once the sole guarantor of minority republican governments, and a source of grievance which hindered long-term acceptance of the Regicide and Revolution by the population at large.

Throughout the rest of the century, then, the first line of defence against invasion and insurrection was not a standing army but the militia: half-trained, modestly equipped, often chaotically organized local defence forces mustered and led by local gentry families appointed by the Crown but not subservient to the Crown. They saw active service or fired shots in anger only as part of the war effort in 1642–5.

There was no police force at all. Few crimes were 'investigated' by the authorities. Criminal trials resulted from accusations and evidence brought by victims or aggrieved parties to the attention of the justices of the peace. Arrests were made by village constables, ordinary farmers or craftsmen taking their turn for a year, or by sheriffs (gentlemen also taking their turn) who did have a small paid staff of bailiffs. Riots and more widespread disorders could only be dealt with by the militia or by a 'posse comitatus', a gathering of freeholders specially recruited for the occasion by the sheriff.

The Crown had little coercive power; it also had little bureaucratic muscle. The total number of paid public officials in the 1630s was under 2,000, half of them effectively private domestic servants of the king (cooks, stable boys, etc.). The 'civil service' which governed England, or at any rate was paid to govern England, numbered less than 1,000. Most remarkable was the smallness of the clerical staff servicing the courts of law and the Privy Council. The volume of information at the finger-tips of decision-makers was clearly restricted by the lack of fact-gatherers and the lack of filing cabinets for early retrieval of the information which was available. In the course of the seventeenth century there was a modest expansion of the civil service with significant improvements in naval administration and in the finance departments (with the emergence of the Treasury as a body capable of establishing departmental budgets and fiscal priorities). Two invaluable by-products of the Civil War itself were the introduction of arabic numerals instead of Roman ones in official accounts and of the printed questionnaire. Although the Privy Council trebled in size in the period 1603–40 and doubled again under Charles II, there was a steady decrease in efficiency, and the introduction of subcommittees of the Council for foreign affairs, trade, the colonies, etc. did not improve on Elizabethan levels of efficiency.

Government in seventeenth century England was by consent. By this we usually mean government by and through Parliament. But, more important, it meant government by and through unpaid, voluntary officials throughout England. County government was in the hands of 3,000 or so prominent gentry in the early seventeenth century, 5,000 or so in the late seventeenth century. They were chosen by the Crown, but that freedom of choice was effectively limited in each county to a choice of fifty or so of the top eighty families by wealth and reputation. In practice all but heads of gentry families who were too young, too old, too mad, or too Catholic were appointed. In the 200 or so corporate boroughs, power lay with corporations of 12–100 men. In most boroughs these men constituted a self-perpetuating oligarchy; in a large minority, election was on a wider franchise. Only in the 1680s was any serious attempt made to challenge the prescriptive rights of rural and urban élites to exercise power.

The significance of the government's dependence on the voluntary support of local élites cannot be overestimated. They controlled the assessment and collection of taxation; the maintenance, training, and deployment of the militia; the implementation of social and economic legislation; the trial of most criminals; and, increasingly, the enforcement of religious uniformity. Their autonomy and authority was actually greater in the Restoration period than in the pre-war period (the Restoration settlement was a triumph for the country gentry rather than for king or Parliament). The art of governing in the seventeenth-century was the art of persuading those who ruled in town and country that there was a close coincidence of interest between themselves and the Crown. For most of the time, this coincidence of interest was recognized. Crown and gentry shared a common political vocabulary; they shared the same conception of society; they shared the same anxieties about the fragility of order and stability. This constrained them to obey the Crown even when it went against the grain. As one gentleman put it to a friend who complained about having to collect possibly illegal taxes in 1625: 'we must not give an example of disobedience to those beneath us'. Local élites were also engaged in endless local disputes, rivalries, conflicts of interest. These might involve questions of procedure or honour; they might involve the distribution of taxation or rates; or promotion to local offices; or the desirability of laying out money to improve highways or rivers. In all these cases the

Crown and the Privy Council was the obvious arbitrator. All local governors needed royal support to sustain their local influence. None could expect to receive that support if they did not co-operate with the Crown most of the time. The art of government was to keep all local governors on a treadmill of endeavour. In the period 1603–40 most governors did their duty even when they were alarmed or dismayed at what was asked of them; after 1660 the terrible memories of the Civil War had the same effect. Only when Charles I in 1641 and James II in 1687 calculatingly abandoned the bargain with those groups with the bulk of the land, wealth, and power, did that coincidence of interest dissolve.

In maintaining that coincidence of outlook we should not underestimate the strength of royal control of those institutions which moulded belief and opinion. The Crown's control of schools and universities, of pulpits, of the press was never complete, and it may have declined with time. But most teachers, preachers, writers, most of the time upheld royal authority and sustained established social and religious views. This is perhaps most clearly seen in the speed with which the ideas of Archbishop Laud and his clique (which, as we shall see, sought to revolutionize the Church of England) were disseminated at Oxford and Cambridge, through carefully planted done in the late seventeenth century than at any other time. strength of divine-right theories of monarchy was far greater in the 1680s amongst the graduate clergy than in the population at large, again as a result of the Crown's control over key appointments in the universities. At the Restoration, the earl of Clarendon told Parliament that Cromwell's failure to regulate schoolmasters and tutors was a principal reason why Anglicanism had thrived in the 1650s and emerged fully-clad with the return of the king: he pledged the government to ensure the political loyalty and religious orthodoxy of all who set up as teachers, and there is evidence that this was more effectively done in the late seventeenth century than at any other time. Even after 1689 when the rights of religious assembly were conceded to Dissenters, they were denied the right to open or run their own schools or academies.

The Early Stuarts

The Crown, therefore, had formidable, but perishable, assets. There was nothing inexorable either about the way the Tudor political system collapsed, causing civil war and revolution, or about the way monarchy and Church returned and re-established themselves. Fewer men feared or anticipated, let alone sought, civil war in the 1620s or 1630s than had done so in the 1580s and 1590s. Few men felt any confidence in the 1660s and 1670s that republicanism and religious fanaticism had been dealt an irrevocable blow.

Throughout Elizabeth's reign, there was a triple threat of civil war: over the wholly uncertain succession; over the passions of rival religious parties; and over the potential interest of the Continental powers in English and Irish domestic disputes. All these extreme hazards had disappeared or receded by the 1620s and 1630s. The Stuarts were securely on the throne with undisputed heirs; the English Catholic community had settled for a deprived status but minimal persecution (they were subject to discriminatory taxes and charges and denied access to public office), while the Puritan attempt to take over the Church by developing their own organizations and structures within it had been defeated. A Puritan piety and zeal was widespread, but its principal characteristic was now to accept the essential forms and practices of the Prayer Book and the canons but to supplement and augment them by their own additional services, preachings, prayer meetings. Above all, they sought to bring a spiritualization to the household that did not challenge but supplemented parochial worship. These additional forms were the kernel and the Prayer-Book services the husk of their Christian witness, but the degree of confrontation between Puritans and the authorities decreased, and the ability of Puritans to organize an underground resistance movement to ungodly kings had vanished. Finally, the decline of internal tensions and the scale of conflicts on the Continent itself removed the incentive for other kings to interfere in England's domestic affairs. In all these ways, England was moving away from civil war in the early seventeenth-century. Furthermore, there is no evidence of a general decline into lawlessness and public violence. Quite the reverse. Apart from a momentary spasm induced by the earl of Essex's attempts to overturn his loss of position at court, the period 1569–1642 is the longest period of domestic peace which England had ever enjoyed. No peer and probably no gentleman was tried for treason between 1605 and 1641. Indeed, only one peer was executed during that period (Lord Castlehavon in 1631, for almost every known sexual felony). The number of treason trials and executions in general declined decade by decade.

Early Stuart England was probably the least violent country in Europe. There were probably more dead bodies on stage during a production of *Hamlet* or *Titus Andronicus* than in any one violent clash or sequence of clashes over the first forty years of the century. Blood feuds and cycles of killings by rival groups were unheard of. England had no brigands, bandits, even groups of armed vagabonds, other than occasional gatherings of 'Moss Troopers' in the Scottish border regions. While the late sixteenth-century could still see rivalries and disputes amongst county justices flare up into fisticuffs and drawn swords (as in Cheshire in the 1570s and Nottinghamshire in the 1590s), respect for the institutions of justice was sufficient to prevent a perpetuation of such violence into the seventeenth century.

Englishmen were notoriously litigious, but that represented a willingness to submit to the arbitration of the king's courts. There was still much rough justice, many packed juries, much intimidation and informal community sanctions against offenders. But it stopped short of killings. A random fanatic stabbed the duke of Buckingham to death in 1628, but few if any other officers of the Crown—lord-lieutenants, deputy lieutenants, justices of the peace, or sheriffs—were slaughtered or maimed in the execution of their duty. A few bailiffs distraining the goods of those who refused to pay rates or taxes were beaten up or chased with pitchforks, but generally speaking the impression of law and order in the early decades is one of the omnicompetence of royal justice and of a spectacular momentum of obedience in the major endeavours of government. It even seems likely that riots (most usually concerned with grain shortages or the enclosure of common land depriving cottagers and artisans of rights essential to the family economy) were declining in frequency and intensity decade by decade. Certainly the degree of violence was strictly limited and few if any persons were killed during riots. The response of the authorities was also restrained: four men were executed for involvement in a riot at Maldon in 1629 just weeks after the quelling of a previous riot. Otherwise, the authorities preferred to deploy minimum force and to impose suspended sentences and to offer arbitration along with or instead of prosecutions. Riots posed no threat to the institutions of the State or to the existing social order.

The fact that few contemporaries expected a civil war may only mean that major structural problems went unrecognized. England may have been becoming ungovernable. Thus, the fact that neither crew nor passengers of an aircraft anticipate a crash does not prevent that crash. But while planes sometimes crash because of metal fatigue or mechanical failure, they also sometimes crash because of pilot error. The causes of the English Civil War are too complex to be explained in terms of such a simple metaphor, but it does seem that the English Civil War was more the consequence of pilot error than of mechanical failure. When, with the wisdom of hindsight, contemporaries looked back at the causes of the 'Great Rebellion' they very rarely went back before the accession of Charles I in 1625. They were probably right.

James I was, in many ways, a highly successful king. This was despite some grave defects of character and judgement. He was the very reverse of Queen Elizabeth. He had a highly articulate, fully-developed, and wholly consistent view of the nature of monarchy and of kingly power—and he wholly failed to live up to it. He was a major intellectual, writing theoretical works on government, engaging effectively in debate with leading Catholic polemicists on theological and political issues, as well as turning his mind and his pen to the ancient but still growing threat of witchcraft, and to the recent and menacing introduction of tobacco. He believed that kings derived their authority directly from God and were answerable to him alone for the discharge of that trust. But he also believed that he was in practice constrained by solemn oaths made at his coronation to rule according to the 'laws and customs of the realm'. However absolute kings might be in the abstract, in the actual situation in which he found himself, he accepted that he could only make law and raise taxation in Parliament, and that every one of his actions as king was subject to judicial review. His prerogative, derived though it was from God, was enforceable only under the law. James was, in this respect, as good as his word. He had several disagreements with his Parliaments, or at any rate with groups of members of Parliament, but they were mostly unnecessary and mostly of temporary effect. Thus he lectured the Commons in 1621 that their privileges derived from his gift, and this led to a row about their origins. But he was only claiming a right to comment on their use of his gift; he was not claiming, and at no point in relation to any such rights and liberties did he claim, that he had the right to revoke such gifts. It was this tactlessness, this ability to make the right argument at the wrong moment that earned him Henry IV of France's *sobriquet*, 'the wisest fool in Christendom'.

His greatest failings, however, were not intellectual but moral and personal. He was an undignified figure, unkempt, uncouth, unsystematic, and fussy. He presided over a court where peculation and the enjoyment of perquisites rapidly obstructed efficient and honest government. Royal poverty made some remuneration of officials from tainted sources unavoidable. But under James (though not under his son) this got out of hand.

The public image of the court was made worse by a series of scandals involving sexual offences and murder. At one point in 1619 a former Lord Chamberlain, a former Lord Treasurer, a former Secretary of State, and a former Captain of the Gentlemen Pensioners, all languished in the Tower on charges of a sexual or financial nature. In 1618, the king's latent homosexuality gave way to a passionate affair with a young courtier of minor gentry background, who rose within a few years to become duke of Buckingham, the first non-royal duke to be created for over a century. Buckingham was to take over the reins of government from the ailing James and to hold them for the young and prissy Charles I, until his assassination in 1628. Such a poor public image cost the king dear. His lack of fiscal self-restraint both heightened his financial problem and reduced the willingness of the community at large to grant him adequate supply.

James I was a visionary king, and in terms of his own hopes and ambitions he was a failure. His vision was one of unity. He hoped to extend the Union of the Crowns of England and Scotland into a fuller union of the kingdoms of Britain. He wanted full union of laws, of parliaments, of churches; he had to settle for a limited economic union, a limited recognition of joint citizenship and for a common flag. The sought-after 'union of hearts and minds' completely eluded him. James's vision was expressed in flexible, gradualist proposals. It was wrecked by the small-mindedness and negative reflexes of the parliamentary county gentry. He also sought to use the power and authority of his three crowns—England, Scotland, and Ireland—to promote the peace and unity of Christian princes, an aim which produced solid achievements in James's arbitration in the Baltic and in Germany in his early years, but which was discredited in his later years by his inability to prevent the outbreak of the Thirty Years War and the renewed conflict in the Low Countries. Finally, he sought to use his position as head of the 'Catholic and Reformed' Church of England, and as the promoter of co-operation between the Presbyterian Scots and episcopal English churches, to advance the reunion of Christian churches. His attempts to arrange an ecumenical council and the response of moderates in all churches, Catholic, orthodox, Lutheran, and Calvinist to his calls for an end to religious strife, were again wrecked by the outbreak of the Thirty Years War. But they had struck a resonant chord in many quarters.

James's reign did see, however, the growth of political stability in England, a lessening of religious passions, domestic peace, and the continuing respect of the international community. His 'plantation policy' in Ulster, involving the dispossession of native Irish Catholic landowners and their replacement by thousands of families from England (many of them in and around Londonderry settled by a consortium of Londoners) and (even more) from south-west Scotland, can also be counted a rather heartless short-term success, though its consequences are all-too-grimly still with us. He left large debts, a court with an unsavoury reputation, and a commitment to fight a limited war with Spain without adequate financial means.

He had squabbled with his Parliament and had failed to secure some important measures which he had propounded to them: of these, the Act of Union with Scotland and an elaborate scheme, known as the Great Contract, for rationalizing his revenues were the only ones that mattered. But he had suffered no major defeat at their hands in the sense that Parliament failed to secure any reduction in royal power and had not enhanced its own participation in government by one jot. Parliament met when the king chose and was dismissed when its usefulness was at an end. Procedural developments were few and had no bearing on parliamentary power. Parliament had sat for less than one month in six during the reign and direct taxation counted for less than one-tenth of the total royal budget. Most members recognized that its very survival as an institution was in serious doubt. No one believed that the disappearance of Parliament gave them the right, let alone the opportunity, to resist the king. James was a Protestant king who ruled under law. He generated distaste in some, but distrust and hatred in few if any of his subjects. Charles I's succession in 1625 was the most peaceful and secure since 1509, and arguably since 1307.

Just as there is a startling contrast between Elizabeth I and James I so there is between James I and Charles I. Where James was an informal, scruffy, approachable man, Charles was glacial, prudish, withdrawn, shifty. He was a runt, a weakling brought up in the shadow of an accomplished elder brother who died of smallpox when Charles was twelve. Charles was short, a stammerer, a man of deep indecision who tried to simplify the world around him by persuading himself that where the king led by example and where order and uniformity were set forth, obedience and peace would follow. Charles I was one of those politicians so confident of the purity of his own motives and actions, so full of rectitude, that he saw no need to explain his actions or justify his conduct to his people. He was an inaccessible king except to his confidants. He was a silent king where James was voluble, a king assertive by deed not word. He was in many ways the icon that James had described in *Basilikon Doron*.

Government was very differently run. Charles was a chaste king who presided over a chaste court; venality and peculation were stanched; in the years of peace after 1629 the budgets were balanced, the administration streamlined, the Privy Council reorganized. In many respects, government was made more efficient and effective. But a heavy price was paid. In part this was due to misunderstandings, to failures of communication. The years 1625–30 saw England at war with Spain (to regain the territories seized from Charles's brother-in-law the elector Palatine and generally to support the Protestant cause) and with France (to make Louis XIII honour the terms of the marriage treaty uniting his sister Henrietta Maria to Charles I). Parliament brayed for war but failed to provide the supply to make the campaigns a success. A mercenary army was sent in vain into Germany; naval expeditions were mounted against French and Spanish coastal strongholds. Nothing was achieved.

The administrative and military preparations themselves, together with financial devices resorted to in order to make good the deficiencies of parliamentary supply, were seen as oppressive and burdensome by many and as of dubious legality by some.

Throughout his reign, however, Charles blithely ruled as he thought right and did little to explain himself. By 1629, king and Parliament had had a series of confrontations over the failure of his foreign policy, over the fiscal expedients needed to finance that policy, over the use of imprisonment to enforce those expedients, and over the king's sponsorship of a new minority group within the Church, whose beliefs and practices sharply diverged from the developing practice and teachings of the Anglican mainstream. In 1629, passions and frustrations reached such a peak that Charles decided that for the foreseeable future he would govern without calling Parliament. He probably believed that if the generation of hotheads and malcontents who had dominated recent sessions was allowed to die off, then the old harmony between king and Parliament could be restored. It was as simplistic as most of his assessments. But the decision was not in itself self-destructive. The three Parliaments of 1625–9 had been bitter and vindictive. But they represented a range of frustrations rather than an organized resistance. They also demonstrated the institutional impotence of Parliament. There was much outspoken criticism of royal policies, but no unity of criticism. Some MPs were anxious about the Crown's religious and foreign policies, others with the legal basis of the fiscal expedients. There was little that men such as John Pym, Sir Edward Coke, Sir Thomas Wentworth, Sir John Eliot, Dudley Digges (to name perhaps the most vociferous royal critics in those sessions) shared in common beyond a detestation of Buckingham and the belief that the misgovernment of the present was best put right by their own entry into office. All were aspirant courtiers both because of the rewards and honours that would flow from office, and because of the principles and policies they would be able to advance. No change of political institutions and no change in the constitution was envisaged. They were not proto-revolutionaries; they lacked the unity of purpose even to stand forth as an alternative government team.

So in the 1630s the king ruled without Parliament and in the absence of any concerted action, peaceful or otherwise, to bring back Parliament. The king raised substantial revenues, adequate for peacetime purposes, and he faced obstruction, and that largely ineffective obstruction, in only one instance—the Ship Money rates used to build a fleet from 1634 onwards. Most of this obstruction was based on local disputes about the distribution of the rate, and over 90 per cent of it was collected, if rather more slowly than anticipated. Arguments about the legality of the measure were heard in open court and after the king's victory payments were resumed at a high level. By 1637 Charles was at the height of his power. He had a balanced budget, effective social and economic policies, an efficient council, and a secure title. There was a greater degree of political acquiescence than there had been for centuries.

He was, however, alienating a huge majority of his people by his religious policies, for his support for Archbishop William Laud was re-creating some of the religious passions of the 1570s and 1580s. But it was not leading to the development of an underground church or of subversive religious activity. Indeed, those who found the religious demands of Laud unacceptable now had an option not available to previous generations: they could and did emigrate to the New World. There, freed from the persecution of the Anglican authorities, they set about persecuting one another in the name of Protestant purity.

There were, however, two things about Laud which dangerously weakened loyalty to the Crown. One was that the teachings of many of those sponsored by the archbishop, and many of the practices encouraged by Laud himself and his colleagues, were reminiscent of Roman Catholic beliefs and ritual. With Laud himself maintaining that the Roman Church was a true church, though a corrupt one, it became widely believed that popery was being let in by a side door, that the Church was being betrayed and abandoned. Laud's own priorities were not, in fact, intended to change the liturgy and observances of the Church, but to restrict Englishmen to a thorough conformity to the letter of the Prayer Book. The 1559 Prayer Book was not only necessary, it was sufficient. Thus the wide penumbra of Puritan practices and observances which had grown up around the Prayer Book was to be curtailed or abolished. This programme incensed all Puritans and worried most other men. Just as bad was Laud's clericism, his attempt to restore the power and authority of the bishops, of the Church courts, of the parish clergy by attacking lay encroachments on the wealth and jurisdiction of the Church. Church lands were to be restored, lay control of tithes and of clerical appointments restricted, the clergy's power to enforce the laws of God enhanced. The most notable visual effect of Laud's archiepiscopate was the removal of the communion tables from the body of the church to the east end, where they were placed on a dais and railed off. At the same time, the rich and ornamental pews set up by the status-conscious clergy were to be removed and replaced by plain, unadorned ones. In the House of God the priest stood at the altar raised above the laity who were to sit in awed humility beneath his gaze. Sinful man could not come to salvation through the word of God alone, or at all, but only through the sacraments mediated by His priesthood. Only a priesthood freed from the greed and cloying materialism of the laity could carry out the Church's mission. Such a programme committed Laud to taking on almost every vested secular interest in the State.

Despite this, in 1637 Charles stood at the height of his power. Yet five years later civil war broke out. Only a catastrophic series of blunders made this possible. The most obvious lesson the king should have learnt from the 1620s (if not the 1590s) was that the Tudor-Stuart system of government was ill-equipped to fight successful wars, with or without parliamentary help. This did not matter since no one was likely to make war on England in the foreseeable future, giving the Crown time in an increasingly favourable economic climate (the great inflation petering out and foreign trade booming). What Charles had to avoid was blundering into an unnecessary war. In 1637, however, he blundered into civil war with his Scots subjects. Governing Scotland from London had proved beyond Charles, whose desire for order and conformity led him first to challenge the autonomy of the Scots lords in matters of jurisdiction and titles to secularized Church lands, and then to attempt to introduce religious reforms into Scotland similar to those advocated by Laud in England. Protests over the latter led to a collapse of order and the king's alternating bluster and half-hearted concession led to a rapid escalation of the troubles. Within twelve months, Charles was faced by the ruin of his Scottish religious policies and an increasing challenge to his political authority there. He therefore decided to impose his will by force. In 1639 and again in 1640 he planned to invade Scotland. On both occasions the Scots mobilized more quickly, more thoroughly, and in greater numbers than he did. Rather than accept a deal with the Short Parliament (April–May 1640) which was willing to fund a campaign against the Scots in return for painful but feasible concessions (certainly for less than the Scots were demanding), Charles preferred to rely on Irish Catholics, Highland Catholics, and specious offers to help from Spain and the Papacy. Poor co-ordination, poor morale, and a general lack of urgency both forced Charles to abandon the campaign of 1639 and allowed the Scots to invade England and to occupy Newcastle in the autumn of 1640. There they sat, refusing to go home until the king had made a treaty with them, including a settlement of their expenses, ratified by an English Parliament.

A unique opportunity thus arose for all those unhappy with royal policies to put things right: a Parliament was called which could not be dismissed at will. The ruthlessness of the way the opportunity was taken was largely the result of that unique circumstance. Within twelve months those institutions and prerogatives through which Charles had sustained his non-parliamentary government were swept away. The men who had counselled the king in the 1630s were in prison, in exile, or in disgrace. But the expected return to peace and co-operation did not occur. Instead, the crisis rapidly deepened amidst ever greater distrust and recrimination. Civil war itself broke out within two years to the dismay and bewilderment of almost everyone. The reasons why Charles's position collapsed so completely, so quickly, and so surprisingly are necessarily a matter of dispute amongst historians. But two points stand out. One is that once the constitutional reforms which were widely desired were achieved, Charles's palpable bad grace, his obvious determination to reverse his concessions at the earliest opportunity, and his growing willingness to use force to that end, drove the leaders of the Commons, and above all John Pym, to contemplate more radical measures. In 1640 almost without exception the members favoured a negative, restrained programme, the abolition of those powers, those prerogatives, those courts which had sustained non-parliamentary government. No one had intended to increase the powers of the two Houses, but only to insist that Parliament be allowed to meet regularly to discharge its ancient duties: to make law, to grant supply, to draw the king's attention to the grievances of the subjects, and to seek redress. By the autumn of 1641 a wholly new view had emerged. It was that the king himself was so irresponsible, so incorrigible, that Parliament, on the people's behalf, had a right to transfer to themselves powers previously exercised by the king. Specifically, this meant that the Houses should play a part in the appointment and dismissal of Privy Councillors and principal officials of State and court, and that the Privy Council's debates and decisions should be subject to parliamentary scrutiny. Such demands were facilitated by the fact that Charles had made very similar concessions to the Scots in his treaty with them in July 1641, and such demands were given new urgency by the outbreak of the Irish rebellion in October.

The Catholics of the north of Ireland, fearful that the English

Parliament would introduce new repressive religious legislation, decided to take pre-emptive action to disarm those Ulster Protestants who would enforce any such legislation. With the legacy of hatred built into the Ulster plantations, violence inevitably got out of hand and something like 3,000 (that is, one in five) of the Protestants were slaughtered. Reports in England credibly suggested even larger numbers. Fatally for Charles I, the rebels claimed to be acting on his authority and produced a forged warrant to prove it. This reinforced rumours of Charles's scheming with Irish Catholics, of his negotiations with Catholic Spain and with the pope for men and money to invade Scotland in 1640, and it followed on from the discovery of army plots in England and Scotland earlier in the year to dissolve Parliament by force. Within weeks it was emphatically endorsed by Charles's attempt, with troops at his back, to arrest five members of the Commons during a sitting of the House. In these circumstances, to entrust Charles with recruiting and commanding the army to subjugate the Irish, an army available for service in England, was unthinkable. John Pym now led a parliamentary attack on Charles I as a deranged king, a man unfit to wield the powers of his office. In the eighteen months before the outbreak of civil war, a majority of the Commons and a minority of the House of Lords came to share that conviction. When Charles I radical constitutional position that they had taken or anticipated taking. But the constitutional dynamic was a limited one. was one which divided the nation.

The first point about the outbreak of the war is, then, that Charles's actions in 1640–2 forced many men into a much more radical constitutional position that they had taken or anticipated taking. But the constitutional dynamic was a limited one. The question of trust arose in relation to an urgent non-negotiable issue: the control of the armed forces to be used against the Irish rebels. This turned attention on a further related question, the king's control of the militia and of those who ran it, the lord-lieutenants and their deputies. These constitutional issues together with the accountability of the king's ministers and councillors to Parliament proved to be the *occasion* of the Civil War. But they were not the prime considerations in the mind of those who actively took sides. Certainly the question of trust drew some men to the side of the Houses; but the palpably new demands now being made by Pym and his colleagues were wholly unacceptable to many others. If the king's flirtations with Popery drove some into the arms of Pym, so Pym drove others into the arms of the king by his reckless willingness to use mass picketing by thousands of Londoners to intimidate wavering members of both Houses to approve controversial measures. But for everyone who took sides on the constitutional issue in 1642, there were ten who found it impossible to take sides, who saw right and wrong on both sides, and who continued to pray and to beg for accommodation and a peaceful settlement. In a majority of shires and boroughs, the dominant mood throughout 1642 was pacifist, neutralist, or at least localist. That is, attempts were made to neutralize whole regions, for demilitarization agreements to be reached between factions or to be imposed by 'peace' movements on both sides, or for the county establishments to impose order and discipline in the name of king or Parliament but without doing anything to further the larger, national war effort. Constitutional issues, however much they pressed them upon those at Westminster who experienced royal duplicity and the London apprentices' politics of menace, were not in themselves weighty enough to start a civil war.

By 1642, however, a second factor was crucial: religion. The religious experiments of Archbishop Laud reactivated Puritan militancy. By 1640 substantial numbers of clergy, of gentry, and especially prosperous farmers and craftsmen had decided that the system of Church government, so easily manipulated by a clique of innovators and crypto-Catholics such as they deemed the Laudians to be, had to be overthrown. The office of bishop must be abolished, the Prayer Book, which, said some, 'is noisome and doth stink in the nostrils of God', must be suppressed, the observance of 'popish' festivals such as Christmas and Easter must be stopped. A majority in Parliament initially favoured a more moderate reform—the punishment of Laud and his henchmen and legislation to reduce the autonomy and jurisdiction of the bishops. But the Scots' pressure for more change, a carefully orchestrated petitioning campaign for reform of the Church 'root and branch', and outbreaks of popular iconoclasm (the smashing of stained glass and the hacking out of communion rails was reported from many regions) led to a rapid polarization of opinion. Since many of those who campaigned against bishops also campaigned against rapacious landlords and against tithes (with implications for property rights in general), the defence of the existing Church became a defence of order and hierarchy in society and the State as well as in religion.

There was an Anglican party before there was a royalist party, and those who rushed to join the king in 1642 were those clearly motivated by religion. On the other side, those who mobilized for Parliament were those dedicated to the overthrow of the existing Church and to the creation of a new evangelical church which gave greater priority to preaching God's word, greater priority to imposing moral and social discipline. It was a vision reinforced by the return of exiles from New England who told of the achievements of the godly in the Wilderness. Like the Israelites of the Old Testament led out of bondage in Egypt to the Promised Land, so God's new chosen people, the English, were to be led out of bondage into a Promised Land, a Brave New World. While the majority of Englishmen dithered and compromised, the minority who took up the armed struggle cared passionately about religion.

Those who hesitated were, then, sucked inexorably into the Civil War. Faced by escalating demands and threats from the minority who had seized the initiative, most men had to choose sides. Many, maybe most, followed the line of least resistance and did what they were told by those in a position immediately to compel obedience. Others, deciding reluctantly and miserably, examined their consciences and then moved themselves and their families to an area under the control of the side which they thought the more honourable. But fear of the king's 'popish' allies and of Parliament's religious zealots made that decision unbearable for many.

The Civil Wars

The first Civil War lasted from 1642 until 1646. It is impossible to say quite when it began: the country drifted into war. In January 1642 the king left London and began a long journey round the Midlands and the north. In April he tried to secure an arsenal of military equipment at Hull (left over from his Scottish campaign). The gates were locked against him and he retired to York. Between June and August, Charles and the two Houses issued flatly contradictory instructions to rival groups of commissioners for the drilling of the militia. This led to some skirmishing and shows of force. By the end of August both sides were recruiting in earnest and skirmishing increased. The king's raising of his standard at Nottingham on 20 August was the formal declaration of war. But the hope on all sides remained either that negotiations would succeed or else that one battle between the two armies now in the making would settle the issue. But that first battle, at Edgehill in South Warwickshire on 23 October, was drawn and settled nothing. Although the king advanced on London and reached Brentford, he did not have the numbers or the logistical support to take on the forces blocking his path. He retreated to Oxford as the winter closed in and the roads became impassable. Only after a winter of fitful peace and futile negotiation did the real war break out. Those first armies had been cobbled together and paid on a hand-to-mouth basis. By the spring, it was clear that the nation had to be mobilized. Armies had to be raised in every region and the money and administrative apparatus to sustain those armies created. The country may have stumbled into war; but the logic of that war and its costs would turn civil disturbance into bloody revolution.

It is probable that at some moments in 1643–5 more than one in ten of all adult males was in arms. No single army exceeded 20,000 men, and the largest single battle—Marston Moor near York in June 1644, which saw the conjunction of several separate armies—involved less than 45,000 men. But there were usually 120,000 and up to 140,000 men in arms during the campaigning seasons of 1643, 1644, and 1645. Both sides organized themselves regionally into 'associations' of counties, each with an army (at least on paper) whose primary duty was to clear the association of enemies and to protect it from invasion. Both sides also had a 'marching army' with national responsibilities. In these circumstances the war was essentially one of skirmishes and sieges rather than of major battles. Some regions saw little fighting (for example, East Anglia, the south coast, mid-Wales); others were constantly marched over and occupied by rival armies (the Severn and Thames valleys were amongst the worst, but the whole of the Midlands was a constant military zone). Parliament's heartland was the area in the immediate vicinity of London. Proximity to the capital and to the peremptory demands of the Houses, and the rapid deployment of thousands of Londoners in arms (the unemployed and the religiously inclined joining up in uncertain proportions) ensured that the lukewarm and the hesitant accepted parliamentary authority. Equally, the king's initial strength lay in the areas he visited and toured: the North and East Midlands in a swathe of counties from Lancashire to Oxfordshire. The far north and the west were initially neutral or confused. Only gradually did royalists gain the upper hand in those areas.

The King had several initial advantages—the support of personally wealthy men, a naturally unified command structure emanating from the royal person, a simpler military objective (to capture London). But Parliament had greater long-term advantages: the wealth and manpower of London, crucial for the provision of credit; the control of the navy and of the trade routes with the result that hard-headed businessmen preferred to deal with them rather than with the king; a greater compactness of territory less vulnerable to invasion than the royalist hinterlands; and the limited but important help afforded by the invasion of 20,000 Scots in 1644 in return for a commitment by the Houses to introduce a form of Church government similar to the Scottish one.

It was always likely that the parliamentary side would wear down the royalists in a long war. So it proved. Purely military factors played little part in the outcome. Both sides deployed the same tactics and used similar weapons; both had large numbers of experienced officers who had served in the armies of the Continental powers in the Thirty Years War. In 1645 both sides 'new modelled' their military organizations to take account of the changing military balance, the king setting up separate grand commands on Bristol and Oxford, Parliament bringing together three separate armies depleted in recent months: an army too large for its existing task, the defence of East Anglia, the unsuccessful southern region army of Sir William Waller, and the 'marching army' of the commander-in-chief, the earl of Essex. This New Model Army was put under the command of an 'outsider', Sir Thomas Fairfax, to avoid the rival claims of senior officers in the old armies, and all MPs were recalled from their commands to serve in the Houses; but otherwise commands were allocated more or less according to existing seniority. The New Model was not, by origin, designed to radicalize the parliamentary cause and it was not dominated by radical officers. Professionalization, not radicalization, was the key; the army's later reputation for religious zeal and for representing a career open to the talents was not a feature of its creation. The great string of victories beginning at Naseby in June 1645 was not the product of its zeal, but of regular pay. In the last eighteen months of the war, the unpaid royalist armies simply dissolved, while the New Model was well supplied. The Civil War was won by attrition.

The last twelve months of the war saw a growing popular revolt against the violence and destruction of war. These neutralist or 'Clubmen' risings of farmers and rural craftsmen throughout west and south-west England sought to drive one or both sides out of their area and demanded an end to the war by negotiation. Again, as the discipline of royalist armies disintegrated they were the principal sufferers. But the hostility of the populace to both sides made the fruits of victory hard to pick.

To win the war, Parliament had imposed massive taxation on the people. Direct taxation was itself set at a level of 15–20 per cent of the income of the rich and of the middling sort. Excise duties were imposed on basic commodities such as beer (the basic beverage of men, women, and children in an age just prior to the introduction of hot vegetable drinks such as tea, coffee, and chocolate) and salt (a necessary preservative in that period). Several thousand gentry and many thousands of others whose property lay in an area controlled by their opponents had their estates confiscated and their incomes employed wholly by the State except for a meagre one-fifth allowed to those with wives and children. By the end of the war, Parliament was allowing less active royalists ('delinquents') to regain their estates on payment of a heavy fine; but the hardliners ('malignants') were allowed no redress and were later to suffer from the sale of their lands on the open market to the highest bidder. All those whose estates were not actually confiscated were required to lend money to king or Parliament; refusal to lend 'voluntarily' led to a stinging fine. In addition to those burdens, both sides resorted to free quarter, the billeting of troops on civilians with little prospect of any recompense for the board and lodging taken. Troops on the move were all too likely to help themselves and to point their muskets at anyone who protested. Looting and pillaging were rare; pilfering and trampling down crops were common. All this occurred in an economy severely disrupted by war. Trade up the Severn was seriously affected by the royalist occupation of Worcester and parliamentarian occupation of Gloucester; or up the Thames by royalist Oxford and parliamentarian Reading. Bad weather added to other problems to make the harvests of the later 1640s

the worst of the century. High taxation and high food prices depressed the markets for manufactures and led to economic recession. The plight of the poor and of the not-so-poor was desperate indeed. The costs of settlement, of the disbandment of armies, and of a return to 'normality' grew.

In order to win the Civil War, Parliament had to grant extensive powers, even arbitrary powers, to its agents. The war was administered by a series of committees in London who oversaw the activities of committees in each county and regional association. Committees at each level were granted powers quite at variance with the principles of common law: powers to assess people's wealth and impose their assessments; to search premises and to distrain goods; to imprison those who obstructed them without trial, cause shown and without limitation. Those who acted in such roles were granted an indemnity against any civil or criminal action brought against them, and (after mid-1647) that indemnity was enforced by another parliamentary committee. Judgments reached in the highest courts of the land were set aside by committee decree. Only thus had the resources to win the Civil War been secured. But by 1647 and 1648 Parliament was seen as being more tyrannical in its government than the king had been in his. The cries for settlement and restoration were redoubled.

In order to win the Civil War, Parliament promised the Scots that the Elizabethan Church would be dismantled and refashioned 'according to the word of God, and the example of the best reformed churches' (a piece of casuistry, since the Scots wrongly assumed that must mean their own church). By 1646 this was accomplished, on paper at least. Episcopacy, cathedrals, Church courts, the Book of Common Prayer and the Kalendar (including the celebration of Christmas and Easter) were abolished and proscribed. In their place a 'Presbyterian' system was set up. Ministers and lay 'elders' from a group of neighbouring churches were to meet monthly to discuss matters of mutual concern. Representatives of all such meetings or 'classes' within each county were to meet regularly. The activities at parish, classical, and provincial level would be co-ordinated by a national synod and by Parliament. No one was exempt from the authority of this new national Church any more than they had been from the old Church. The new national faith would be based upon a new service book ('the Directory of Public Worship', emphasizing extempore prayer and the preaching of the Word), new catechisms, and new articles of faith. At every level, the 'godly' were to be empowered to impose moral duties, a 'reformation of manners', and strict spiritual observance through ecclesiastical and secular sanctions. But this Puritan experiment was stillborn. It gave the laity far too much control to please many strict Presbyterian ministers. It gave too little authority to the individual parishes and too much to classes, provinces, and synods to please many others. The precise doctrinal, liturgical, and disciplinary requirements were too rigid for others or just plain unacceptable in themselves. While there was 'Puritan' unity in 1642 against the existing order, the imposition of one particular alternative created a major split in the movement. Many 'Independents' refused to accept the package and began to demand liberty of conscience for themselves and a right of free religious assembly outside the national Church. Some began to refuse to pay tithes. The disintegration of Puritanism preceded any attempt to impose the Presbyterian system. At the same time, this system was bitterly opposed by the great majority of ordinary people. Over four generations they had come to love the Prayer Book and the celebration of the great Christian festivals. They resented the loss of both, and also the Puritan doctrine that forbade anyone to come to receive holy communion without first being approved by the minister and his self-righteous henchmen and given a certificate of worthiness. Throughout much of England, therefore, including East Anglia, the decrees against the Prayer Book and the celebration of Festivals were a dead letter. Ministers who tried to impose change were opposed and even thrown out, and although one in five of the clergy were ejected by parliamentary commissions for spiritual, moral, or political unfitness, a majority of their replacements sought secret episcopal ordination. The Puritan experiment was ineffective but added to popular hatred of an arbitrary Parliament.

But if the great majority, even on the winning side, became convinced that the Civil War had solved nothing and had only substituted new and harsher impositions on pocket and conscience for the old royal impositions, a minority, equally dismayed by the shabby realities of the present, persuaded themselves that a much more radical transformation of political institutions was necessary. God could not have subjected his people to such trials and sufferings without a good purpose. To admit the futility of the struggle, to bring back the king on terms he would have accepted in 1642, would be a betrayal of God and of those who had died and suffered in His cause. Once again it was the religious imperative which drove men on. Such views were to be found in London, with its concentration of gathered churches and economic distress, and in the army, with its especially strong memories of suffering and exhilaration, many soldiers aware of God's presence with them in the heat of battle. Furthermore a penniless Parliament, bleakly foreseeing the consequences of seeking to squeeze additional taxes from the people, enraged the army in the spring of 1647 by trying to disband most of them and to send the rest to reconquer Ireland without paying off the arrears of pay which had been mounting since the end of the war. In the summer of 1647 and again in the autumn of 1648 a majority in the two Houses, unable to see the way forward, resigned themselves to accepting such terms as the king would accept. His plan since his military defeat, to keep talking but to keep his options open, looked likely to be vindicated.

On both occasions, however, the army prevented Parliament from surrender. In August 1647 it marched into London, plucked out the leading 'incendiaries' from the House of Commons, and awed the rest into voting them the taxation and the other material comforts they believed due to them. In doing so, they spurned the invitation of the London-based radical group known as the Levellers to dissolve the Long Parliament, to decree that all existing government had abused its trust and was null and void, and to establish a new democratic constitution. The Levellers wanted all free-born Englishmen to sign a social contract, an Agreement of the People, and to enjoy full rights of participation in a decentralized, democratic state. All those who held office would do so for a very short period and were to be accountable to their constituents. Many rights, above all freedom to believe and practice whatever form of Christianity one wanted, could not be infringed by any future Parliament or government. The army, officers and men, were drawn to the Levellers' commitment to religious freedom and to their condemnation of the corruption and tyranny of the Long Parliament, and officers and 'agitators' drawn from the rank and file debated Leveller proposals, above all at the Putney debates held in and near Putney Church in November 1647. But the great majority finally decided that the army's bread-and-butter demands were not to be met by those proposals. Instead the army preferred to put pressure on the chastened Parliament to use its arbitrary powers to meet their sectional interests.

The outcome was a second Civil War, a revolt of the provinces against centralization and military rule. Moderate parliamentarians, Clubmen, whole county communities rose against the renewed oppressions, and their outrage was encouraged and focused by ex-royalists. The second Civil War was fiercest in regions little affected by the first war, insufficiently numbed by past experience—in Kent, in East Anglia, in South Wales, in the West and North Ridings. It was complicated by the king's clumsy alliance with the Scots, who were disgusted by Parliament's failure to honour its agreement to bring in a Church settlement like their own, and who were willing, despite everything, to trust in vague assurances from the duplicitous Charles. If the revolts had been co-ordinated, or at least contemporaneous, they might have succeeded. But they happened one by one, and one by one the army picked them off. With the defeat of the Scots at Preston in August, the second Civil War was over.

It had solved nothing. Still the country cried out for peace and for settlement, still the army had to be paid, still the king prevaricated and made hollow promises. As in 1647, the Houses had to face the futility of all their efforts. By early December there were only two alternatives: to capitulate to the king and to bring him back on his own terms to restore order and peace; or to remove him, and to launch on a bold adventure into unknown and uncharted constitutional seas. A clear majority of both Houses, and a massive majority of the country, wanted the former; a tiny minority, spearheaded by the leaders of the army, determined on the latter. For a second time the army purged Parliament. In the so-called Pride's Purge, over half the members of the Commons were arrested or forcibly prevented from taking their seats. Two-thirds of the remainder boycotted the violated House. In the revolutionary weeks that followed, less than one in six of all MPs participated, and many of those in attendance did so to moderate proceedings. The decision to put the king on trial was probably approved by less than one in ten of the assembly that had made war on him in 1642.

In January 1649, the king was tried for his life. His dignity and forbearance made it a massive propaganda defeat for his opponents. His public beheading at Whitehall took place before a stunned but sympathetic crowd. This most dishonourable and duplicitous of English kings grasped a martyr's crown, his reputation rescued by that dignity at the end and by the publication of his self-justification, the *Eikon Basilike*, a runaway best seller for decades to come.

Commonwealth and Protectorate

From 1649 to 1660 England was a republic. In some ways this was a revolutionary period indeed. Other kings had been brutally murdered, but none had previously been legally murdered.

Monarchy was abolished, along with the House of Lords and the Anglican Church. England had four separate constitutions between 1649 and 1659, and a chaos of expedients in 1659–60. Scotland was fully integrated into Britain, and Ireland subjugated with an arrogance unprecedented even in its troubled history. It was a period of major experiment in national government. Yet a remarkable amount was left untouched. The legal system was tinkered with but was recognizably the old arcane common law system run by an exclusive legal priesthood; local government reverted to the old pattern as quarter sessions returnd to constitute veritable local parliaments. Exchequer reasserted its control over government finance. Existing rights of property were protected and reinforced, and the social order defended from its radical critics. There was a loosely structured national Church. If no one was obliged to attend this national Church, they were required to pay tithes to support its clergy and to accept the secular and moral authority of parish officers in the execution of the duties laid upon them in Tudor statutes. In practice, the very freedom allowed to each parish in matters of worship, witness, and observance, permitted Anglican services and the Anglican feasts to be quietly and widely practised.

Institutionally, it was indeed a decade of uneven progress back towards a restoration of monarchy. From 1649 to 1653, England was governed by the Rump Parliament, that fragment of the Long Parliament which accepted Pride's Purge and the Regicide and which assumed unto itself all legislative and executive power. Despite the high-minded attempts of some MPs to liken themselves to the assemblies of the Roman Republic, the Rump in practice was a body that lived from hand to mouth. Too busy to take bold initiatives and to seek long-term solutions, let alone to build the new Jerusalem, the Rump parried its problems. By selling the Crown's lands, Church lands, and royalist lands, it financed the army's conquest of Ireland, which included the storming of Drogheda and Wexford and the slaughtering of the civilian population, acts unparalleled in England, but justified as revenge for the massacres of 1641, and its gentler invasion of Scotland. By the establishment of extra-parliamentary financial institutions and by the restoration of pre-war forms of local government, the Rump wooed enough men in the provinces into acquiescence to keep going and to defeat the royalists in a third Civil War. By incoherent and contradictory pronouncements on religion, it kept most men guessing about its ecclesiastical priorities, and drove none to desperate opposition. The Rump even blundered into a naval war with the Dutch and captured enough Dutch merchantmen in the ensuing months to double Britain's entrepôt trade. A demoralized royalist party licked its wounds and tried to pay off its debts; a dejected majority of the old parliamentarian party grudgingly did what they were told but little more. The Rump stumbled on.

By the spring of 1653 the army was ready for a change. With fresh testimonies of divine favour in their victories in Scotland and Ireland and over Charles II at the battle of Worcester, its leaders, above all its commander (since 1649) Oliver Cromwell, demanded the kind of godly reformation which the Rump was too preoccupied and too set in its ways to institute.

Disagreements between Rumpers and army commanders led finally to the peremptory dissolution which the latter had ducked in 1647 and 1648. Fearful that free elections would provoke a right-wing majority, Cromwell decided to call an 'assembly of saints', a constituent assembly of 140 hand-picked men drawn from amongst those who had remained loyal to the godly cause, men who shared little beyond having what Cromwell called 'the root of the matter in them', an integrity and intensity of experience of God's purpose for his people, whose task it was to institute a programme of moral regeneration and political education that he hoped would bring the people to recognize and to own the 'promises and prophecies' of God. Cromwell's vision of 140 men with a fragment to contribute to the building up of a mosaic of truth was noble but naïve. These 140 bigots of the Nominated or Barebones Parliament, leaderless and without co-ordination, bickered for five months and then, by a large majority, surrendered their power back into the Lord General's hands. Cromwell's honest attempts to persuade others to govern while he stood aside had failed. The army alone propped up the republic and could make and break governments. The army must be made responsible for governing.

From December 1653 until his death in September 1658, Oliver Cromwell ruled England as Lord Protector and Head of State. Under two paper constitutions, the *Instrument of Government* (1653–7, issued by the Army Council) and the *Humble Petition and Advice* (1657–8, drawn up by a Parliament), Cromwell as head of the executive had to rule with, and through, a Council of State. He also had to meet Parliament regularly. Cromwell saw himself in a position very similar to that of Moses leading the Israelites to the Promised Land. The English people had been in bondage in the Land of Egypt (Stuart monarchy); they had fled and crossed the Red Sea (Regicide); they were now struggling across the Desert (current misfortunes), guided by the Pillar of Fire (Divine Providence manifested in the army's great victories, renewed from 1656 on in a successful war against Spain). The people, like the Israelites, were recalcitrant and complaining. Sometimes they needed to be frog-marched towards the Promised Land, as in 1655–6 when Cromwell became dismayed by the lack of response in the people at large during an abortive royalist uprising (few royalists participated but many turned a blind eye, and few beyond the army rushed to extinguish the flames of rebellion). He then instituted a system of government placing each region under the supervision of a senior military commander. These 'Major Generals' were responsible for security but also interfered in every aspect of local government and instituted a 'reformation of manners' (a campaign of moral rearmament). At other times Cromwell tried to wheedle the nation towards the Promised Land with policies of 'healing and settling', playing down the power of the sword and attempting to broaden participation in government and to share power with local magistrates and with Parliament.

If Cromwell had settled for acquiescence and a minimum level of political acceptance, he could have established a secure and lasting regime. But he yearned for commitment and zeal, for a nation more responsive to the things of God, more willing to obey His commands. Cromwell was an orthodox Calvinist in his belief in the duty of God's elect to make all men love and honour Him, and in his belief that God's providence showed His people the way forward. He was unusual in believing that, in this fallen world, the elect were scattered amongst the churches. Toleration was a means to the end of restoring the unity of God's word and truth. This religious radicalism went along with a social conservatism. The hierarchical ordering of society was natural and good, its flaws and injustices not intrinsic but the consequence of sin. It was not society but man's behaviour within society that must be reformed.

By executing Charles, Cromwell cut himself off from justifications of political authority rooted in the past; by acknowledging that a free vote of those who held the franchise would restore the king, that is by refusing to base his authority on consent, Cromwell cut himself off from arguments of the present. His self-justification lay in the future, in the belief that he was fulfilling God's will. But because he believed that he had such a task to perform, he had a fatal disregard for civil and legal liberties. To achieve the future promised by God, Cromwell governed arbitrarily. He imprisoned men without trial. When George Cony, a merchant, refused to pay unconstitutional customs duties, Cromwell imprisoned him and his lawyer to prevent him taking his case to court. When Parliament failed to make him an adequate financial provision, he taxed by decree. When the people would not respond voluntarily to the call to moral regeneration, he created Major-Generals and set them to work. Hence the supreme paradox. Cromwell the king-killer, the reluctant head of state, the visionary, was begged by his second Parliament to become King Oliver. He was offered the

Crown. Ironically he was offered it to limit his power, to bind him with precedents and with the rule of law. Because such restrictions were irrelevant to the task he believed he was entrusted to perform, because God's Providence did not direct him to restore the office that He had set aside, he declined the throne.

While Cromwell lived, the army (who had the immediate military muscle) and the country gentry (who had the ultimate social authority) were kept in creative tension. Cromwell was a unique blend of country gentleman and professional soldier, of religious radical and social conservative, of political visionary and constitutional mechanic, of charismatic personal presence and insufferable self-righteousness. He was at once the only source of stability and the ultimate source of instability of the regimes he ran. If he could have settled for settlement, he could have established a prudent republic; if he had not had a fire in his belly to change the world, he would never have risen from sheep farmer to be head of state. With his death, the republic collapsed. His son lacked his qualities and succumbed to the jealousy of the senior military commanders. They in turn fell out amongst themselves and a national tax strike hastened the disintegration of the army. Eighteen months after Cromwell's death, one section of the army under General Monck decided that enough was enough. Free elections were held and Charles II was recalled.

Restoration Monarchy

Charles was restored unconditionally. His reign was declared to have begun at the moment of his father's death; those Acts of Parliament to which his father had assented were in force, all the rest were null and void (which meant, for example, that all Crown and Church land sold off by the republic was restored, but also that those royalists who had paid fines or who had repurchased their estates under Commonwealth legislation went uncompensated). Parliament assured itself of no greater role in the government than it had possessed under Elizabeth and the early Stuarts (except for a toothless act requiring a triennial session of Parliament, an Act Charles II ignored without popular protest in 1684). Since the Long Parliament and those of the Interregnum had abused their authority as freely as Charles I had done, it seemed pointless to build them up as a counterpoise to the Crown. Rather the Restoration Settlement sought to limit royal power by handing power back from the centre to the localities. Charles I had agreed to the abolition of the prerogative courts, to the restriction of the judicial power of the Privy Council (now emasculated and thus unable to enforce policy), to the abolition of prerogative taxation. The local gentry were freer than ever before to run their own shires. What is more, with remarkable nerve and courage, Charles set out to build his regime on as broad a base as possible. He refused to give special positions of favour and trust to his own and his father's friends. There was to be power-sharing at every level of government: in the council and in the distribution of office at court, in the bureaucracy, in local government. Old royalists, old parliamentarian moderates who had shunned the Interregnum regimes, Cromwellian loyalists, all found places. Indeed, the group who did least well were the royalist exiles. Charles defeated parliamentary attempts at a wide proscription and punishment of the enemies of monarchy. Only those who signed Charles I's death warrant and a handful of others were exempted from the general Act of Indemnity and Oblivion (one bitter cavalier called the Restoration an 'act of indemnity to the King's enemies and of oblivion to his friends'). It took courage to determine that it was better to upset old friends (who would not send the king on his travels again) than to upset old enemies. Plots against Charles II were few and restricted to radical religious sects. Even a government with less than 3,000 men in arms could deal with such threats.

Charles had hoped to bring a similar comprehensiveness to the ecclesiastical settlement. He sought to restore the Church of England, but with reforms that would make it acceptable to the

majority of moderate Puritans. To this end, he offered bishop-
rics to a number of such moderates and he issued an interim
settlement (the Worcester House Declaration) which weakened
the power and autonomy of the bishops and made the more
contentious ceremonies and phrases of the Prayer Book op-
tional. He also wanted to grant freedom of religious assembly
(if not equality of political rights) to the tiny minority of Puritans
and Catholics who could not accept even a latitudinarian
national Church. For eighteen months he fought for this moderate settlement only to be defeated by the determination of the
rigorist Anglican majority in the Cavalier Parliament, by the
lukewarmness of his advisers, and by the self-destructive behaviour of Richard Baxter and the Puritan leaders. They refused the senior positions in the Church offered them, they
campaigned against toleration, and they persisted in unreason-
able demands at the conference held to reform the Prayer Book.
Their Scottish colleagues, more flexible and pragmatic, achieved
a settlement acceptable to a majority of their brethren.

Charles finally abandoned the quest for a comprehensive
Church and assented to the Act of Uniformity which restored
the old Church, lock, stock, and barrel, and which imposed a
number of stringent oaths and other tests on the clergy. In
consequence about one in five of the clergy were ejected by the
end of 1662, and many of them began to set up conventicles
outside the Church. Charles then set about promoting the cause
of religious toleration for all non-Anglicans. Even though his
first attempt in January 1663 was a failure, he had the consola-
tion of knowing that he had reversed traditional roles. The
pre-war Puritans had looked to Parliament for protection from
the king; the new non-conformists had to look to him for
protection from Parliament. For fifteen years this made his
position in relation to the majority of them politically safe.
None the less, it was the single greatest weakness of the Restoration settlement. A comprehensive political settlement was
set against a narrow, intolerant religious settlement. Few local
governors were Dissenters; but many were sympathetic to them

and reluctant to impose the full strictures of the vindictive laws which Parliament went on to pass against their religious assemblies.

In general, Charles's problems did not arise from the settlement but from his preferred lines of policy. In some ways, he was a lazy king. His adolescence and early manhood had been dominated by the desire to gain the throne and once he had returned from exile all his ambition was spent. He was the only one of the Stuarts not to be a visionary, not to have long-term goals. This made it easy for him to back down whenever his policies were strongly opposed. But while he lacked vision, he did not lack prejudices and preferences. He was a man with a strong rationalist streak—a worldly man with many mistresses and seventeen acknowledged bastards, a cynic with regard to human nature, an intellectual dilettante who took a lively if spasmodic interest in the affairs of the Royal Society launched at his accession. But this intellectual empiricism was joined with an emotional and spiritual mysticism which he got from his parents. He believed that he possessed semi-divine powers and attributes (no king touched so much for the king's evil, that class of unpleasant glandular and scrofulous disorders that kings were reputed to be able to cure). He was also strongly drawn to Roman Catholicism. His mother, wife, brother, and favourite sister were all Catholics and while he had a *bonhomie* which made him accessible to many, it was superficial, and he was only really close to his family. He knew that wherever Catholicism was strong, monarchy was strong. The Catholics had remained conspicuously loyal to his father. If any theology of Grace made sense to Charles it was Catholic doctrine (of his mistresses, Charles said that he could not believe that God would damn a man for taking a little pleasure by the way). He was drawn to Catholicism and twice revealed that preference (in a secret treaty with France in 1670 and in his deathbed reception into the Catholic Church). He was much too sensible politically to declare himself except on his deathbed. But it did lead him to make clear his commitment to toleration. Both this and his obvious admiration for his cousin Louis XIV of France caused growing alarm in England.

Charles was given a generous financial settlement in 1660–1 (£1.2 million per annum), principally from indirect taxation. Bad housekeeping made this inadequate in his early years, and in general it left him with little flexibility. He had no ability to raise emergency taxation without recourse to Parliament and limited access to long-term credit. Thus although Charles had sole responsibility for foreign policy and for making war and peace, Parliament clearly would not vote the necessary revenues without a consideration of the cause for which the money was needed.

The period needed a great administrative reformer in the mould of Henry VIII's Thomas Cromwell, and it did not find one. Decision-making and policy enforcement needed restructuring and formalizing. The Council was too large and amorphous to be effective, and decisions were too often made at one *ad hoc* meeting in the king's chambers and unmade at a subsequent *ad hoc* meeting. This led to real uncertainty and eventually to panic about who was in charge. With the Council emasculated, enforcement of policy was left to individual ministers and departments without co-ordination. Patronage was chaotically handled. Equally, Parliament was inefficient and increasingly crotchety. Charles, feeling that those elected in 1661 were as loyal a group of royalists as he was likely to meet, kept the 'Cavalier' Parliament in almost annual sessions for eighteen years. In part, its inefficiency was due to a growing rivalry between the two Houses, especially over the Lords' claim to take over much of the jurisdiction of the defunct conciliar courts, and a number of sessions were wrecked by deadlock on such issues. In part, its inefficiency was due to there being no government programme for it to get its teeth into. A body of several hundred members without recognized leadership spent much time discussing what to discuss. With most senior ministers in the Lords, and a predisposition to resist management by the court, the 1660s and 1670s were years of drift. Charles ruled without serious threat to his position at home or abroad. The early euphoria gave way to a mild political depression as the final ravages of plague, the humiliating Dutch incursions up the Medway during the second Dutch war (1665–7), and the Great Fire of London (1666) sapped the self-confidence of 1660–1 that God would bless a land that had come to its senses.

There were many political embarrassments, such as the defeat of a major attempt to introduce religious toleration (1672–3), the suspension of interest payments on his loans (1672), and the political brawls in Parliament as the discredited ministers of the 'Cabal' administration blamed each other for their collective failure (1674–5). But the only challenge to his authority came in the Exclusion crisis of 1678–81. This was triggered by the revelations of Titus Oates, Israel Tonge, and other desperadoes of a popish plot to murder Charles and put his Catholic brother on the throne. This was more lucid and more plausible than many similar tales, but was just as mendacious. The mysterious death of an investigating magistrate and the discovery of conspiratorial letters in the possession of James's private secretary also heightened tension. The result was a full-scale attempt to place a parliamentary bar on the accession of James and thereby to shatter Charles's divine-right theories of government.

In fact the political leaders of the Exclusion movement were at least as concerned to use the crisis to clip Charles's wings as James's. For the first twelve months their target was not James but Charles's Cavalier-Anglican chief minister, the earl of Danby. This appears odd, but it is clear that Shaftesbury, the leader of the Opposition, saw Danby's regime as just as much a threat to liberties as James might be. Danby's principles were the very antithesis of Shaftesbury's, in that he had developed sophisticated techniques of parliamentary management, had centralized financial control, had upset the balance of interests in local government to the advantage of Cavalier-Anglicans, seemed willing to develop a standing army in peacetime, and had allied with the Dutch against the French. Shaftesbury, a turncoat in the Civil War, a member of Barebones Parliament and of Cromwell's council of state, who had served Charles as Chancellor of the Exchequer and Lord Chancellor, had a consistent record of supporting free and unfettered Parliaments, decentralization, religious toleration, a horror of standing armies, and a distaste for the Dutch. Danby's policies amounted in fact to nothing more than a programme to give Charles II a quiet life: to Shaftesbury it looked like incipient absolutism. By now there was such a conjunction in people's minds between Popery and arbitrary government, that even Danby could be portrayed as a secret agent of the papists, despite his impeccable Anglicanism. Only when Danby was imprisoned in the Tower did Shaftesbury turn to Exclusion, as an end in itself and as a means to other ends. These included shattering the theoretical basis of divine right and creating the need for continued political action and cohesion (to secure Exclusion on Charles's death, for James would hardly accept it without a fight). To secure Exclusion, Shaftesbury created the first political party in English history. His 'Whigs' produced a mass of propaganda, organized petitions and demonstrations, and co-ordinated campaigns in three successive general elections (1679–81).

They failed. Charles held all the trump cards. The Whigs were fatally divided over who should take James's place as heir—Monmouth, the favoured royal bastard, or Mary, James's Protestant daughter. Almost without exception, the Whigs were committed to lawful, peaceful action only. The memories of civil war were too strong to allow violent councils to hold sway. Charles could, and did, use his power to summon and dissolve Parliament to his own advantage; he had a solid majority in the House of Lords that would vote down the Exclusion Bill time after time; a trade boom enhanced royal revenues on trade and freed Charles from financial worry; and his policy of offering concessions short of Exclusion bought off many moderates. Shaftesbury fatally assumed that Charles would weaken under pressure. He never grasped that Charles would always concede matters of policy, but never matters of principle. He would never have surrendered his divine right. His ultimate sacrifice would have been to divorce the barren queen he respected if he did not cherish, to remarry, and to solve the succession crisis via the marriage bed. It would have been the supreme demonstration of his political style.

As it was, the same iron nerve, pragmatism, and easy good-will to all, which he had demonstrated in 1660, won him the day. A nation racked by political deadlock for three years backed off, took stock, and rallied to him. In his last years he was able to pick off those who had crossed him, reward those who had stood by him, enjoy a quiet life at last. He left a nation governed by and for those who believed in the divine right of kings, the divine right of the Church of England, and the divine right of the localities to run their own affairs. The complacency of the Tory-Anglicans knew no bounds, as they welcomed James II to the throne, the king whose rights they had protected. Such complacency was in for a rude shock.

James was in fact a bigot. His government of Scotland in the early 1680s had seen a most severe repression and extensive use of judicial torture against Protestant Dissenters ('conventiclers'). Worse still, James believed himself to be a moderate. He had no deliberate plan to set himself up as an absolutist king on the Continental model. But since a trade boom greatly enhanced royal revenues (and his first Parliament, meeting under threat of a military bid for the throne by Charles's favoured bastard, the duke of Monmouth, voted higher rates in addition), he was able to maintain an army of 20,000 men. The army's most striking characteristic was its professionalism and the apolitical views of its career commanders. James had twice urged Charles to use his tiny army to get rid of troublesome Parliaments. He would not have hesitated to use his army against a recalcitrant assembly, but he did not intend to rule without Parliament. Indeed, at the time of his fall, he was engaged in the most elaborate operation ever attempted, to 'pack' Parliament with sympathizers. Until early 1688 James's second marriage, more than a decade old, was childless. James—already fifty years old—expected to be succeeded by his Protestant daughter Mary and her Dutch husband, William of Orange. He intended to secure for all time a religious and civil equality for his co-religionists. This meant not only removing from them all the penalties and disabilities under the Penal Laws (fines for non-attendance at Anglican worship) and Test Acts (barring them from all offices and paid employments under the Crown), but also allowing the Catholic Church to be set up alongside the Anglican Church. This meant establishing a Catholic hierarchy and diocesan structure and public places of worship. It also meant allowing Catholics a share in the universities (maybe even the take-over—or 'restoration'—of some colleges to serve as Catholic seminaries). It would probably have led on to granting Catholics exemption from tithes and the authority of Anglican courts. James honestly believed that once the ban on Catholic evangelism was lifted, once the civil and religious disabilities were removed, the return of hundreds of thousands to the Faith was certain. He believed that this granting of 'equal status' to Catholics was a humane and moderate programme. If, in the short term, a certain amount of positive discrimination was necessary to favour Catholics in appointments to national and local office, this too was only fair as a correcting exercise.

It need hardly be said that the Tory-Anglican political nation was outraged. Their loyalty to the Church proved greater than their loyalty to their anointed king. James soon discovered that no Tory-Anglican Parliament would repeal the anti-Catholic legislation and while a packed judiciary would uphold his suspension of that legislation, it would come back into force the moment he died and his Protestant heir took over. He therefore made a desperate bid to jettison the Tory squirearchy and to build an alternative power base in an alliance of Catholics and Protestant Dissenters. Three-quarters of all JPs were sacked, together with most lord-lieutenants. The new men were of lower social origin, and James's purge constituted a greater social revolution in local government than had been attempted even in the years 1646–60. James called in the charters of most towns and reorganized their governments to give Dissenters control (this was especially vital if he was to get a sympathetic parliamentary majority). To win over the Dissenters, a Declaration of Indulgence was issued giving them full religious freedom.

The Tory-Anglicans were stung, but initially pacific. The whirlwind would blow itself out; James would die and Mary succeed him; they would take their revenge. Passive disobedience would limit James's success. Thus seven bishops petitioned him explaining why they would not obey his order to instruct their clergy to read the Declaration of Indulgence to their flocks. They also committed the Church to a future Anglican toleration of Protestant Dissenters. James had the bishops tried for seditious libel, but even his judges summed up against him and they were acquitted. However, the Tory complacency of 1687 ('we are not to be laughed out of our doctrine of Non-Resistance and passive obedience on all occasions' wrote the marquis of Halifax) turned to stunned horror in June 1688 with the birth of a son and heir to James II. Now indeed the possibility of a dynasty of rabid Catholics appeared to stretch out before them.

Ironically, while many Anglican leaders came to put their religion before their political principles, many Dissenters chose to put political principles first. They had little doubt that James was using them for present purposes only. Thus leaders of both parties joined in the desperate expedient of inviting William of Orange to come to England, suitably protected with armed men, to remonstrate with James. Perhaps they really believed that this would lead to James agreeing to William's humiliating terms: the recall of the writ designed to produce a packed Parliament and new writs to return a 'free' Parliament; a declaration of war on France; and a commission to investigate the legitimacy of the infant Prince of Wales. Only a minority were willing to join William's invasion by taking up arms; but even fewer were willing to lift their little fingers to help James.

Whatever those who invited William may have expected, William himself almost certainly intended to depose James. He was taking a quite outrageous risk, justified only by the necessity of harnessing the whole of Britain's military, naval, and financial resources to the struggle against Louis XIV. But how he expected to secure the throne is less clear. In the event, he was able to get himself proclaimed joint ruler with Mary within a matter of weeks because James had what can only be called a complete mental collapse. His army and William's never met. William landed at Torbay on 5 November and moved east. James brought his army as far as Salisbury where incessant nosebleeds held him up. As his behaviour became more and more bizarre and manic, many of his professional officers and commanders deserted him. James then fled back to London and was quickly in William's hands. Even then, his position was not hopeless. A series of vague undertakings and promises would have ensured that he retained the loyalty of most peers and leading gentry. But he was beyond reason. He twice escaped (on the first occasion, to William's annoyance, being captured on the Kent coast by well-meaning fishermen and sent back). His flight to France, the public promises of Louis XIV to use French arms to restore him, and William's clear statement that he would not protect the realm unless he shared the throne with his wife, left the political nation no choice. Almost all Whigs and most Tories, rationalizing their conduct as best they could, and in a variety of ways, agreed that James had vacated his throne and that the Crown be offered jointly to William and Mary. The Glorious Revolution of 1688 was even more unanticipated and unplanned than the Great Rebellion of 1642; its consequences probably more momentous.

Had the English Revolution had any lasting effects on the power of the Crown? The answer is that it had surprisingly little. In the 1680s the Crown was far better endowed financially, it had a growing but still inadequate civil service, and an unprecedented opportunity to create a standing army. Parliaments had shown themselves quite unable to defeat the king, in the sense of imposing on him restrictions and conditions that he disliked or taking away from him powers he had hitherto enjoyed. The royal prerogatives in the 1680s were little different from those of the 1600s. The king could veto bills he did not approve; he could dispense individuals from the operation of statutes; he could pardon whomsoever he chose. He selected his own councillors, judges, senior administrators, and he could dismiss most of them at will. He was not bound to take anyone's advice. If he had lost most of his feudal revenues and his 'discretionary' powers to raise money, he had been amply compensated by parliamentary taxes, some in perpetuity, others for life.

The only really major weakening of royal power had come in the legislation of 1641 which abolished those courts and councils which were particularly susceptible to royal control. The most important restriction was the one which took away from the Privy Council its judicial power. Its teeth removed, the Council ceased to be an executive, active body, monitoring, cajoling, and directing the work of local government, and reverted to what it had begun as: a talking shop, a place where the king sought advice. It probably never functioned as well under the Stuarts as under the Tudors; James I allowed factionalism to spill over from the Council to the floor of Parliament; Charles I did not want to hear alternative proposals from groups within the Council. He wanted puppets to confirm his own preconceptions. Charles II enjoyed policy-making in secret, summoning ministers to hasty meetings in his private quarters, so that no one knew what was going on. For different reasons, each of these monarchs encouraged the growth of secret committees of the Council comprising the holders of key offices. Here was the seed of the Cabinet councils of the eighteenth century. Other conciliar courts abolished in 1641 included Star Chamber, High Commission, Requests, and—more by chance than design—the Regional Councils of the north and in the marches of Wales. Charles II was restricted at the Restoration not by the gentry in Parliament, but by the gentry in the provinces. Almost all the methods by which Tudor and early

Stuart kings could bring recalcitrant county communities to heel had been taken away. Government was more than ever by their active consent. In the 1660s all taxation except the customs, all ecclesiastical legislation (such as the Act of Uniformity, the Conventicle Acts, and the Five Mile Act), and most security matters, were entrusted to the gentry magistrates with no appeal from their decisions to the central courts.

The abolition of the monarchy and the experience of republican rule thus had a very limited direct impact. Even the memory of Charles I's public trial, conviction, and decapitation did not change the monarchy's pretensions to rule by divine right nor make them more respectful of Parliaments. After all, the political nation knew that regicide had cost them dear, that it had added to, rather than removed, their oppressions. The problems of matching resources to responsibilities had become clearer; but the problems themselves had neither increased nor diminished. The alternatives for England were to see either a strengthening of the central executive and administration at the expense of the independent county gentry; or else a further withering away of the centre, turning England into a series of semi-autonomous county-states, self-governing, undertaxed, stagnant. The latter was the preference of a range of 'Country parties' visible in the Parliaments of the 1620s, the neutralist groups in the Civil War, and many Whigs in the 1670s and 1680s. It was also the preference of republicans such as John Milton, who admired the Dutch republic and longed to see the same oligarchic civic humanism develop in England. Most dramatically, it was the ideal of democratic groups such as the Levellers, who wanted to make governors more accountable, government subservient to the liberties of a sovereign people, and who therefore urged devolution of power to elected local magistrates and juries. But these 'Country' ideologies were incompatible with the development of a global empire. The expansion into the West Indies and along the eastern seaboard of North America (from Carolina to the St. Lawrence); into extensive trade networks with South America, West Africa, India, and Indonesia; even the protection of the vital trades with the southern and eastern Mediterranean all required strong naval and military power. This could only be sustained by a massive increase in the ability of the State to tax and to wage war. It was the combined threat of Louis XIV and the exiled James II after 1689 to introduce Popery and arbitrary government which finally forced through the necessary constitutional and political changes, as the following chapter will show. The Stuart century was one of unresolved tensions.

Intellectual and Religious Life

For the Church of England, if not for the monarchy, the seventeenth century was an age of disillusionment. By the time of the Glorious Revolution of 1688–9 it had lost the intellectual, moral, spiritual authority it had acquired by 1603. Intellectually, Anglicanism was on the offensive at the beginning of the century. The generation living through the events of 1559 witnessed a settlement cobbled together to meet political necessities, a hybrid of Protestant doctrine and Catholic practice. The criticisms of the first generation of Puritans were the more telling because their Marian exile allowed them to speak from experience of the purity of the Continental reformed churches. The new generation of the 1590s and 1600s had known no other Church, and had come to love the rhythms of the Anglican liturgical year and the cadences of Cranmer's liturgy. The work of Jewel, Hooker, and Andrewes presented the Church of England as the best of all Churches, claiming an apostolic descent and an uninterrupted history from the Celtic Church which gave it a greater authority than the schismatic Protestant Churches, and a superiority over Rome in that it had sloughed off the corruptions and failings of the Roman Catholic Church just as it had sloughed off the usurped authority of the bishops of Rome. The Church of England had an authority as ancient and as apostolic as Rome's, and a practice more true to the injunctions of Christ. These were claims which the Puritans did not find easy to meet.

Puritans displayed an increasing willingness to work within the Church. Their response to James I's accession, the Millenary Petition, called only for modifications within the existing framework. At the Hampton Court Conference of 1604, in which James presided over a meeting of bishops and Puritans, discussion was entirely about how to make the episcopal national Church more effectively evangelical. Puritans yearned for a godly prince who, like the Emperor Constantine 1,200 years before, would bring good order to his State, and promote and protect true religion. They chafed for more to do, rather than for less. They worked within the Church and not against it. Even the 5 per cent of the nation who made up the Catholic recusants succumbed to an intellectual onslaught led by Anglican divines. The greatest single debate on any issue in the first quarter of the century was over the duties of Catholics to take the oath of allegiance and to eschew papal claims to command their political allegiance. Anglican arguments prevailed and the Catholics, while holding to their faith, abandoned political resistance. The Gunpowder plot was the last real popish plot. As English Catholicism became controlled less by militant clergy and more by a prudent peerage and gentry, its pacifism and political acquiescence grew.

Protestant unity, if not uniformity, was retained until the Long Parliament. Puritans added their own practices to those of the Church, but the number who opted out and set up conventicles or assemblies in defiance of the Church was extremely few. Some hundreds, perhaps thousands, moved to New England rather than submit to the narrow interpretation of Anglican practice required by Archbishop Laud. But there was no schism.

The Civil War and Interregnum years saw the disintegration not only of Anglicanism, but of English Puritanism. The structure of the Church of England was abolished (bishops, church courts) or proscribed (the Prayer Book, the celebration of Christmas or Easter). Cathedrals were turned into preaching centres or secularized (used as barracks, prisons, shopping arcades). In thousands of parishes the old services and celebrations were carried on despite the proscriptions. But the Church leaders lost their nerve. The bishops fled, hid, remained silent. They were not replaced as they died. By 1660 the survivors were all over seventy years of age, and Church of England bishops were an endangered species.

But those who dreamed of replacing Anglicanism by a Calvinist church like those of Massachusetts, Scotland, or Geneva were disappointed. The Presbyterian system conceived by Parliament was stillborn. The chaos of the Civil War created a bewildering variety of sects and gathered churches. The Baptists, one of the few strong underground churches before 1640, spread widely via the army. Many new groups denied Calvinist notions of an Elect predestined to salvation, and proclaimed God's Grace to be freely available. Some even proclaimed universal salvation. Such groups were most evident in London and other provincial cities. The largest of all the sects was the Quakers, whose informal missionary evangelism in the countryside gained thousands of adherents in the 1650s: denouncing the formalization of religion, and the specious authority of 'hireling priests' in their 'steeple houses', the Quakers urged men to find the divine spark within themselves, the Holy Spirit which came direct to the Christian, mediated neither by the Church nor Scripture. Their hatred of formal worship and of tithes led them into widespread campaigns of militant passive disobedience. One of their leaders, James Nayler, was tried for blasphemy by the second Protectorate Parliament in 1656. Although he escaped the sentence of death, he was subject to a variety of severe physical punishments, Parliament taking several hours to contemplate which bits of him should be sliced or cut off.

There was no recovering the old triumphalism after 1660. The Church might be outwardly restored to its ancient forms at the Restoration, but it had neither the self-assurance nor the power to reimpose a general uniformity. Anglican apologetic was defensive and edgy. With the disappearance of High Commission and the rust of disuse settled in its diocesan courts, it lacked the weapons to punish defaulters. The ignominy of its abolition left it institutionally enfeebled. In 1660 the celebration of Easter and the ubiquitous return of maypoles may have been spontaneous and have shown signs of its deep roots in popular culture. But those who chose to defy it were not going to be forced back into its assemblies. The decision in 1662 not to broaden its appeal by adapting its liturgy and by softening episcopal pretensions drove two thousand clergy out of the Church. Despite the attempts to prevent unlawful conventicles, the Baptists, Quakers, and other radicals were not to be up-rooted. Even more important, the tens of thousands of 'Dissenters' of 1662 who were within the moderate Puritan tradition re-examined whether their desire to be part of a national Church (though not the one on offer) outweighed their desire for a pure worship of God. In the 1580s and the 1600s they had preferred to 'tarry for the magistrate', to stay in the Church and to wait for better times. In Restoration England, they came more and more to opt for separation. In the early seventeenth century they found 'much piety in Babylon'; now they abandoned such temporizing and went into schism. The Toleration Act of 1689 was the formal recognition of the fact of religious pluralism. Unable to punish those who were not its members, and unable to compel men and women to be its members, the Church of England was a spent spiritual force.

In the early and mid-seventeenth century, most intellectuals and most governors believed that there was a divine imperative to bring godliness, good discipline, and order to the English nation. God was guiding His people towards a Promised Land of peace and justice in which men would love and worship him as it was their duty to do. The vision of a better world that could be built by man's response to the divine challenge was shared by James and Charles I, by Wentworth and Laud, by Pym and Cromwell. All political writings were suffused by the immanence of God in his Creation, by a deep sense of God's activity in human history and in His providences, His signs of Himself. Shakespeare's plays, Donne's poems, the thoughts of

Henry Parker and the young John Milton all proclaim the same point: the plays of Marlowe are the exceptions that prove the rule.

No such hopes survived the Interregnum. The trauma of regicide left few royalists with faith in the providences of God; the much deeper sense of betrayal experienced by the radicals in 1660 largely explains their political quiescence thereafter. Psychologically, the pain of betrayal after such visible testimonies of divine favour was too great. Instead, most of the Puritans and their heirs internalized the kingdom of God. They accepted the world as the domain of sin and of imperfectibility. Within this vale of tears, each person must seek personal peace by building a temple of grace within himself or herself. This acceptance of the limits of what Church and State could achieve dominated the ideology of the late seventeenth century. It is apparent in the way Charles II's jaundiced view of the world was combined with his deep personal mysticism, in the latitudinarianism of the bishops and of the clerical establishment; in the Dissenters' abandonment of the quest for a national Church. A few men continued to seek the millennium (Sir Isaac Newton combined his successful search for physical laws with an unsuccessful search for the dating of the Second Coming from the runes in the Book of Revelation), but most settled for making the most of things as they were. John Milton heroically confronted a God who appeared to have guided his people in the 1640s and 1650s only to betray them in 1660. *Paradise Lost* looked at the Omnipotent Creator who let man fall, *Paradise Regained* looked at the temptation of Christ in the wilderness, at the false worldly ways in which Man might proclaim the gospel. Perhaps republicans had been tempted into the wrong paths. *Samson Agonistes*, most poignantly of all, studied a man given great gifts by God who failed to use them in His service. Just as Samson dallied with Delilah and was shorn of his strength, so the republicans had been distracted by the things of the flesh in the 1650s and had missed their chance to do God's will. But the more typical Puritan work of the Restoration is

Bunyan's *Pilgrim's Progress* which concerns the individual's personal search for peace and salvation.

Christianity was being depoliticized and demystified. The characteristic Anglican tracts of the late seventeenth century had titles like *The Reasonableness of Christianity* and *Christianity not Mysterious*. Where God had been in the very warp and woof of nature and life, he now became the creator who set things going, and the spirit who worked within the individual and kept him obedient to moral rules. Sermons stressed the merits of neighbourliness and charity. Ministers were encouraged to preach that religious duties meant being kind to old people and animals rather than preaching about the transformation of the world. From the Dissenting side, John Locke, pleading for religious toleration, defined a church as a voluntary society of men, meeting together to worship God in such fashion as they deemed appropriate. Religion had become an unthreatening matter, almost a hobby. The authorities need not concern themselves with what consenting adults did in private meetings. The Puritans of previous generations could not have conceived anything so anaemic.

This dilution of religious energies, this breakdown of a world-view dominated by religious imperatives can be seen in literature and in science. Restoration theatre differs from Jacobean not in its vulgarity or even in its triviality so much as in its secularism. Metaphysical poetry, which rooted religious experience in the natural world, gave way to a religious poetry either more cerebral and coolly rational, or else more ethereal and other-worldly.

Secularization was also an aspect of change in the visual arts. Tudor and Stuart country houses emphasized paternalistic Christian values, being built around a great hall in which the household and a wider community gathered to do business and to eat together. There might be a 'high table', reflecting hierarchy and degree, but there was an easy informality of social relations. By the late seventeenth century, new houses had 'withdrawing' rooms and private dining-rooms, while servants and other members of the household were given separate quarters. Houses were set in spacious parks surrounded by high walls and patrolled by gamekeepers. Royal palaces showed the way in these developments.

The seventeenth century, like the sixteenth, saw little church building. Perhaps a majority of all new churches were those needed in London after the Great Fire of 1666. There was, however, a stark contrast between the intensity and devotional emphasis of early Stuart churches and chapels such as the one at Peterhouse, Cambridge, and the coolness, light, rationalist air of Wren's London churches. Allegorical stained glass and dark wood panelling gave way to marble. The recumbent effigies of souls at rest gave way to an upright statuary of men and women reflecting on their moral duties.

In all the visual arts, the influence of the Counter-Reformation art of Spain, Spanish Italy, Spanish Netherlands—an ornateness that bound together the natural and the supernatural worlds—gave way to the influences of Louis XIV's France—self-indulgent, revelling in its own material extravagance. In the early seventeenth century, artists, musicians, and poets joined forces to produce the Masque, an entertainment that sought to bring together the world of classical civilization and Christian values, of audiences drawn into the action as performers, a merging of fantasy and reality. The power of the illusion was so great in the case of Inigo Jones and Ben Jonson's Masques for Charles I, that the king came to believe that his own piety and virtue would soon infect his subjects and that order and uniformity could be as easily achieved in the State as on the stage. No such illusion bedevilled the artifice of the opera, the equivalent art-form of the late seventeenth century. While early Stuart writers wrestled with the heroic and the tragic, late Stuart writers turned to the domesticated homiletics of the novel and to the mock epics of Dryden and later of Pope.

Restoration science was just as secularized. In the 1640s and 1650s, scientists had sought what they termed 'a great instauration'. Drawing on the ideas of Francis Bacon, and led by visionary social engineers such as Samuel Hartlib and the Bohemian exile Comenius, the scientific establishment were lionized by the Puritan politicians and undertook to build a Brave New World. Man would tame and gain dominion over the natural world. Medical advances would vanquish disease, agricultural advances would conquer hunger and want. The reformation of justice and of education would bring man into peaceful enjoyment of the new order. It was yet another facet of Protestant eschatology, and the scientific Zion, like other Zions, evaporated in 1660. The later seventeenth century in the Royal Society was not an age of visions but of piecemeal enquiry and improvement. Francis Bacon's principles of exact observation, measurement, and of inductive reasoning, refined by the Frenchman Descartes, allowed major advances in the classification and study of plant and animal life. Harvey's discovery of the circulation of the blood, just before the Civil War, led on to a series of advances in the knowledge of anatomy and physiology in the second half of the century. Isaac Newton's *Philosophiae Naturalis Principia Mathematica* (1687) was the basis of understanding of the physical laws for two hundred years, and the work of Robert Boyle in chemistry and Robert Hooke in geology created new disciplines on the basis of extensive experimentation and measurement. The advance of the physical sciences hit hard at the older mysteries. The discovery of the geometrical movement of heavenly bodies destroyed the credibility of astrology in intellectual circles. It is astonishing how quickly the discovery of natural laws bred a confidence that *everything* had a natural explanation. The realm of magic, of witches and spells, was abandoned by the educated. Within a generation of 1640 the prosecution of witches almost ceased. This was not because the people at large ceased to believe in curses and in magic, but because it was impossible to secure convictions from sceptical judges and jurors. Science and technology did not in fact advance on all fronts. The economy remained almost wholly dependent on human and animal muscle-power. No progress was made towards harnessing

FURTHER READING

1. THE TUDOR AGE

GENERAL WORKS

John Guy, *Tudor England* (Oxford, 1988), the most up-to-date and comprehensive account of the period.

P. Williams, *The Tudor Regime* (Oxford, 1979), the most enlightened general survey of Tudor government.

C. S. L. Davies, *Peace, Print and Protestantism, 1450–1558* (London, 1976), a lucid introduction especially useful on social and economic history.

G. R. Elton, *Reform and Reformation: England 1509–1558* (London, 1977), the best-informed account of the early Tudors.

G. Donaldson, *All the Queen's Men: Power and Politics in Mary Stewart's Scotland* (London, 1983), an encyclopaedic who's who.

J. Wormald, *Court, Kirk and Community, 1470–1625* (London, 1981), the best survey of early modern Scotland.

D. M. Palliser, *The Age of Elizabeth: England under the Later Tudors, 1547–1603* (London, 1983), the best synthesis of social and economic conditions.

D. M. Loades, *The Tudor Court* (London, 1986), a solid anatomy of the political and cultural focus of the State.

BIOGRAPHIES

S. B. Chrimes, *Henry VII* (London, 1972), a sound synthesis of recent research.

J. J. Scarisbrick, *Henry VIII* (London, 1968), an enthralling and original biography accepted as standard.

E. W. Ives, *Anne Boleyn* (Oxford, 1986), a lively introduction to the factional politics of Henry VIII's reign.

A. F. Pollard, *Wolsey* (London, 1929), a dated but indispensable work.

R. Marius, *Thomas More* (London, 1985), the best biography.

D. M. Loades, *The Reign of Mary Tudor* (London, 1979), a solid but essential conspectus.

C. Read, *Mr. Secretary Cecil and Queen Elizabeth, Lord Burghley and Queen Elizabeth* (London, 1955, 1960), a two-volume study valuable on diplomacy, but which pays insufficient attention to domestic patronage and faction.

P. Johnson, *Elizabeth I: a Study in Power and Intellect* (London, 1974), a fair-minded assessment by a professional biographer, but Elizabeth's influence is overrated.

STUDIES OF SPECIAL TOPICS

G. R. Elton, *Reform and Renewal: Thomas Cromwell and the Common Weal* (Cambridge, 1973), the most convincing portrait of Thomas Cromwell by the leading authority.

A. G. Dickens, *The English Reformation* (London, 1964), a dispassionate and comprehensive account.

J. Loach and R. Tittler (eds.), *The Mid-Tudor Polity* (London, 1980), a provocative collection of essays by revisionist historians.

P. Collinson, *The Elizabethan Puritan Movement* (London, 1967), an authoritative study by the acknowledged expert.

C. Haigh (ed.), *The Reign of Elizabeth I* (London, 1984), revisionist essays on the reign.

G. Mattingley, *The Defeat of the Spanish Armada* (London, 1959), an absorbing book by a writer who knew Spanish as well as English sources.

L. Stone, *The Crisis of the Aristocracy* (Oxford, 1965), an important if controversial study of Tudor high society.

K. Thomas, *Religion and the Decline of Magic* (London, 1971), a sparkling and original study of the mentality of Tudor Englishmen.

R. Strong, *The Cult of Elizabeth: Elizabethan Portraiture and Pageantry* (London, 1977), a cultural backcloth by the leading expert.

M. James, *Society, Politics and Culture* (Cambridge, 1986), related case-studies tracing the social, political, and cultural roots of conformity and obedience in the State.

C. Haigh (ed.), *The English Reformation Revised* (Cambridge, 1987), incorporates the recent historiography on the Reformation.

2. THE STUARTS

POLITICAL AND CONSTITUTIONAL HISTORY

B. Coward, *The Stuart Age* (London, 1980), the best introductory survey.

A. B. Worden (ed.), *Stuart England* (London, 1986).

C. Russell, *The Crisis of Parliaments 1509–1660* (Oxford, 1971).

D. Hirst, *Authority and Conflict 1603–1658* (London, 1985).

J. R. Jones, *Country and Court 1658–1714* (London, 1979).

F. M. G. Higham, *Catholic and Reformed: A Study of the Church of England 1559–1662* (London, 1962), excellent study of religious thought.

J. P. Kenyon, *The Stuarts* (London, 1958).

S. J. Houston, *James I* (London, 1973).

R. Ollard, *The Image of the King: Charles I and Charles II* (London, 1979).

J. Miller, *James II: A Study in Kingship* (London, 1978).

J. S. Morrill, *The Revolt of the Provinces* (London, 1976).

A. Woolrych, *Battles of the English Civil War* (London, 1961).

G. E. Aylmer, *The Levellers in the English Revolution* (London, 1975), a brief essay and key texts.

C. Hill, *The World Turned Upside Down* (Harmondsworth, 1973), re-creates the world of the religious radicals of the 1650s.

C. H. Firth, *Oliver Cromwell and the Rule of the Puritans* (Oxford, 1900).

J. P. Kenyon, *The Popish Plot* (London, 1972).

J. R. Jones, *The Revolution of 1688 in England* (London, 1972).

G. Donaldson, *Scotland: James V to James VII* (Edinburgh, 1965).

T. W. Moody, F. X. Martin, F. J. Byrne (eds.), *A New History of Ireland*, vol. iii 1534–1691 (Oxford, 1976), a long narrative.

M. MacCurtain, *Tudor and Stuart Ireland* (Dublin, 1972) a short analysis.

SOCIAL, ECONOMIC, CULTURAL

D. C. Coleman, *The Economy of England 1450–1750* (Oxford, 1977), a brilliantly crisp synthesis.

K. Wrightson, *English Society 1580–1680* (London, 1982), re-creates the mental world of the seventeenth-century villager.

C. Clay, *Economic Expansion and Social Change: England 1500–1700* (Cambridge, 1984).

P. Laslett, *The World We Have Lost* (London, 1971).

L. Stone, *The Crisis of the Aristocracy* (abridged version, Oxford, 1967).

J. Hook, *The Baroque Age* (London, 1976).

R. Strong, *Van Dyck: Charles I on Horseback* (London, 1972).

C. Webster, *The Great Instauration* (London, 1970).

K. V. Thomas, *Religion and the Decline of Magic* (London, 1971).

M. Spufford, *Small Books and Pleasant Histories: Popular Fiction and its Readers in 17th Century England* (London, 1981).

C. Hill, *Society and Puritanism in Pre-Revolutionary England* (London, 1964).

J. Bossy, *The English Catholic Community 1570–1850* (London, 1975).

T. C. Smout, *A History of the Scottish People 1560–1830* (London, 1969).

DOCUMENTS AND CONTEMPORARY TEXTS

Samuel Pepys, *Diary*, various editions, but all previous ones superseded by that of R. C. Latham and W. Matthews, 11 vols. (London, 1970–83).

The Illustrated Pepys, ed. R. C. Latham (London, 1978), a marvellous sampler.

John Evelyn, *Diary*, various editions and extracts, principally the edition by E. S. de Beer, 6 vols. (Oxford, 1955).

J. Aubrey, *Brief Lives* (again many editions but e.g. Harmondsworth, 1962).

R. Gough, *The History of Myddle* (Harmondsworth, 1981), a splendid evocation of life in a seventeenth-century parish, written by a local farmer.

J. P. Kenyon, *The Stuart Constitution* (Cambridge, 1962), for texts and stimulating commentary.

J. Thirsk and J. P. Cooper, *Seventeenth-century Economic Documents* (Oxford, 1972).

BIBLIOGRAPHY

M. F. Keeler, *Bibliography of British History: Stuart Period, 1603–1714* (Oxford, 1970), a comprehensive guide to publications up to 1960.

J. S. Morrill, *Critical Bibliographies in Modern History: Seventeenth Century Britain* (Folkestone, 1980), complements Keeler and offers comments on the works discussed.

CHRONOLOGY

* Entries in *italics* denote events belonging to the history of the Roman Empire.

	Marcus Aurelius (*161–80*); *major wars on the Danube*
? c.163	Hadrian's Wall restored
193	Clodius Albinus proclaimed in Britain
	Severan Emperors (193–235)
196–213	Britain becomes two provinces
208–11	Campaigns of Septimius Severus and Caracalla in Scotland
235–70	*Imperial crisis: civil wars and invasions in East and West*
260–73	'Gallic Empire'
270s	Renewed growth in Britain
	Diocletian (284–305)
	'The Tetarchy'
287–96	Carausius and Allectus
296	Britain recovered by Constantius
after 296	Britain becomes a civil diocese of four provinces
	House of Constantius (305–63)
306	Campaign of Constantius I in Scotland; Constantine the Great proclaimed at York
324	*Constantine sole emperor; foundation of Constantinople*
340–69	Period of severe stress: internal troubles, harassment by barbarians
350	*Magnentius proclaimed in Gaul*
353	*Constantius II sole emperor*
353	Purge by Paul the Chain
	House of Valentinian (364–92)
367–9	'Barbarian Conspiracy', recovery and restoration of Britain by the elder Theodosius
	House of Theodosius (379–455)
	Theodosius the Great (379–95)
383	Magnus Maximus proclaimed in Britain; victory over Picts
	Honorius (395–423)
398–400	Victories over Picts, Scots, Saxons
400–2	Possible troop withdrawals by Stilicho
402/3	*Western imperial court withdrawn from Milan to Ravenna*
406	Britain revolts from Honorius: two emperors proclaimed

407	Constantine III proclaimed in Britain
	Constantine III rules from Arles (407–11)
409	Britain revolts from Constantine III: end of Roman rule in Britain
410	'Rescript of Honorius': letter to Britons (?), significance disputed
429	St. Germanus visits Britain
c.450	The *adventus Saxonum*: Hengest and Horsa settle in Kent (traditional date)
455	Hengest rebels against Vortigern (traditional date)
477	Saxon settlement of Sussex (traditional date)
495	Saxon settlement of Wessex (traditional date)
c.500	Battle of *Mons Badonicus*
560	Æthelberht, later over-king, becomes king in Kent
577	The West Saxons capture Gloucester, Cirencester and Bath
597	St. Augustine's mission arrives in Kent
616	Raedwald of East Anglia, as over-king, makes Edwin king of Northumbria
c.624	Death of Raedwald, and his probable burial in the Sutton Hoo barrow
627	Conversion of Edwin and the Northumbrian court
633	Battle of Heavenfield; Oswald of Northumbria becomes over-king
635	Conversion of King Cynegils of Wessex
642	Oswald is killed at Oswestry by King Penda of Mercia
655	Penda is defeated and killed at the *Winwaed* by Oswy of Northumbria, who becomes over-king
664	Synod of Whitby
669	Arrival of Archbishop Theodore
672	Synod of Hertford; battle of the Trent, marking the beginnings of the rise of Mercia
685–8	Expansion of Wessex under Caedwalla to include Kent, Surrey and Sussex
716	Æthelbald become king of Mercia
731	Bede completes his *Ecclesiastical History*
746–7	First Council of Clofesho
757	Death of Æthelbald; Offa becomes king of Mercia
786	Legatine Council held under Offa

793–5	Danish raids on Lindisfarne, Jarrow, and Iona
796	Death of Offa
825	Egbert of Wessex defeats Mercia and annexes Kent, Essex, Surrey, and Sussex
835	Big Danish raid on Kent
865	The Danish 'Great Army' lands
867	Northumbria falls to the Danes
870	East Anglia falls to the Danes; murder of St. Edmund
871	The Danes attack Wessex; Alfred becomes king
874	Mercia falls to the Danes
878	(March) The Danes drive Alfred into the Somerset marshes
	(May) Alfred defeats the Danes at Edington; Guthrum is baptized
899	Death of Alfred; Edward 'the Elder' becomes king of Wessex
910–20	Edward and Æthelflaed reconquer most of the Danelaw
919	Norse kingdom of York is founded by Raegnald
924	Death of Edward; Athelstan becomes king
937	Athelstan defeats the Norse, Scots and Strathclyde Welsh at Brunanburh
939	Death of Athelstan; Edmund become king
940	Dunstan begin to refound Glastonbury as a regular monastic house
946	Death of Edmund
954	The last king of York is deposed
959	Edgar becomes king
960	Dunstan becomes Archbishop of Canterbury
c.970	*Regularis Concordia* is compiled
973	Edgar is crowned and consecrated, and receives the submission of British princes
975	Death of Edgar; Edward 'the Martyr' becomes king
979	Murder of Edward; Æthelred 'the Unready' becomes king
991	The Danes defeat Alderman Byrhtnoth and the Essex levies at Maldon; treaty between England and Normandy
1002	Æthelred orders the massacre of all Danes in England

1003	Danish invasion led by King Swein
1013	Swein returns with a new army; the Danelaw accepts him as king
1014	Swein dies; the Danish army in England elect Cnut as their king
1016	(April) Æthelred dies; Edmund 'Ironside' becomes king
	(autumn) Cnut defeats Edmund at Ashingdon; Edmund dies and Cnut becomes King of all England
1017	Cnut divides England into four earldoms
1035	Death of Cnut
1037	Harold becomes king
1040	Death of Harold; Harthacnut becomes king
1042	Death of Harthacnut; Edward 'the Confessor' becomes king
1051–2	Conflict between King Edward and Godwin earl of Wessex
1053	Death of Godwin; his son Harold becomes earl of Wessex
1064–5	Earl Harold visits Duke William in Normandy
1066	(January) Death of King Edward; Earl Harold becomes king
	(September) King Harold of England defeats and kills King Harold of Norway at Stamford Bridge
	(October) Duke William of Normandy defeats and kills King Harold of England at Hastings

VOL. 2 THE MIDDLE AGES

1066	(December) William is consecrated king
1067–70	English rebellions
1069–70	The harrying of the north
1086	Domesday Survey carried out
1087	Death of William I; accession of William II Rufus
1088	Rebellion in support of Robert Curthose
1093	Anselm appointed Archbishop of Canterbury
1096	Robert pawns Normandy ot Rufus
1100	Death of William Rufus; accession of Henry I
1101	Invasion of Robert Curthose
1106	Battle of Tinchebray; Curthose imprisoned; Henry I takes Normandy
1107	Settlement of Investiture Dispute in England

1120	Wreck of the White Ship
1128	Marriage of Empress Matilda to Geoffrey of Anjou
1135	Death of Henry I; accession of Stephen
1139–53	Civil war in England
1141	Battle of Lincoln; Stephen captured; later exchanged for Robert of Gloucester
1141–5	Geoffrey of Anjou conquers Normandy
1149	Cession of Northumbria to David of Scotland
1152	Henry of Anjou (later Henry II) marries Eleanor of Aquitaine
1153	Henry invades England; he and Stephen come to terms
1154	Death of Stephen; accession of Henry II
1157	Henry regains Northumbria
1162	Becket appointed Archbishop of Canterbury
1164	Council and Constitutions of Clarendon; Becket goes into exile
1166	Assize of Clarendon
1169–72	English conquest of Ireland begins
1170	Coronation of the young king; murder of Becket
1173–4	Rebellion against Henry II; William 'the Lion' (king of Scotland) invades the north
1183	Death of the young king
1189	Death of Henry II; accession of Richard I
1190–92	Richard I on crusade
1193–4	Richard in prison in Germany
1193–1205	Hubert Walter, Archbishop of Canterbury (justiciar 1194–8; chancellor 1199–1205)
1197	Death of Rhys of Deheubarth
1199	Death of Richard I; accession of John; establishment of Chancery Rolls
1203–4	Philip Augustus conquers Anjou and Normandy
1208–14	Interdict in England
1214	Battle of Bouvines: French victory
1215	Magna Carta; civil war in England
1216	Louis (later Louis VIII) invades; death of John; accession of Henry III
1217	Battles of Lincoln and Dover; Louis withdraws
1221–4	Arrival of Dominican and Franciscan Friars in England
1224	Louis VIII completes conquest of Poitou

1232	Dismissal of Hubert de Burgh
1240	Death of Llywelyn the Great
1254	Henry III accepts papal offer of throne of Sicily
1258	Barons take over royal government; provisions of Oxford
1259	Treaty of Paris between England and France
1264	Battle of Lewes; Henry III captured; government of Simon de Montfort
1265	Battle of Evesham; killing of Simon de Montfort
1267	Henry recognizes Llywelyn ap Gruffydd as Prince of Wales
1272	Death of Henry III; accession of Edward I
1276–7	First Welsh War
1282–3	Edward's conquest of Wales
1286–9	Edward I in Gascony
1291	Edward I asserts his overlordship over Scotland
1294	War with France begins
1295	Franco-Scottish alliance
1296	Edward I invades Scotland; his conflict with the Church
1297	Edward I's conflict with his magnates; his expedition to Flanders
1306	Rebellion of Robert Bruce
1307	Death of Edward I; accession of Edward II
1314	Scottish victory at Bannockburn
1315–16	Great famine
1321–2	Civil war in England
1327	Deposition and death of Edward II; accession of Edward III
1330	Edward III takes the reins of government
1337	The Hundred Years War begins
1339–41	Political crisis in England
1346	English victories at Crécy and Neville's Cross
1347	English capture Calais
1348	First occurrence of plague in England
1356	English victory at Poitiers
1361	Second major occurrence of plague
1376	'Good Parliament' meets; death of Edward, the Black Prince
1377	Death of Edward III; accession of Richard II

1381	The Peasants' Revolt
1382	Condemnation of John Wycliffe's works
1388	'Merciless Parliament' meets; battle of Otterburn against the Scots
1389	Richard II declares himself of age
1394–5	Richard II's expedition to Ireland
1396	Anglo-French treaty
1397–9	Richard II's 'tyranny'
1399	Deposition of Richard II; accession of Henry IV
1400	Rebellion of Owain Glyndŵr begins (to 1410)
1403	Henry Hotspur defeated at Shrewsbury
1405	Execution of Archbishop Scrope of York
1408	Defeat of the earl of Northumberland at Bramham Moor
1413	Death of Henry IV; accession of Henry V
1415	English victory at Agincourt
1419–20	English conquest of Normandy
1420	Anglo-French treaty of Troyes
1422	Death of Henry V; accession of Henry VI
1435	Death of John, duke of Bedford; Franco-Burgundian treaty of Arras
1436–7	Henry VI comes of age
1445	Henry VI marries Margaret of Anjou
1449–50	French overrun Normandy
1450	Murder of the duke of Suffolk; John Cade's rebellion
1453	French overrun Gascony; Henry VI becomes ill
1455	Battle of St. Albans between Richard, duke of York and the royalist forces
1459	Defeat of the duke of York at Blore Heath and Ludford Bridge
1461	Deposition of Henry VI; accession of Edward IV
1465	Capture of Henry VI
1469	Rebellion of Richard, earl of Warwick and George, duke of Clarence
1470	Deposition of Edward IV; return of Henry VI
1471	Return of Edward IV; death of the earl of Warwick at Barnet; death of Henry VI
1475	Edward IV's expedition to France; Anglo-French treaty of Picquigny

1477	William Caxton's first printed book in England
1483	Death of Edward IV; accession, deposition, and death of Edward V; accession of Richard III; rebellion of Henry, duke of Buckingham
1485	Death of Richard III at Bosworth; accession of Henry VII

VOL. 3 THE TUDORS AND STUARTS

1487	Rebellion of Lambert Simnel
1491	Birth of Prince Henry
1509	Accession of Henry VIII
1510	Execution of Empson and Dudley
1512	War with France and Scotland
1513	Battle of Flodden: English victory over Scotland
1515	Wolsey appointed Lord Chancellor
1522	War with France
1525	Peace with France
1527	Divorce crisis begins
1528	War with Spain
1529	Peace of Cambrai; fall of Wolsey: Sir Thomas More succeeds as Lord Chancellor
1532	More resigns
1533	Henry VIII marries Anne Boleyn; Act of Appeals; birth of Princess Elizabeth
1534	Act of Supremacy
1535	Execution of More and Fisher
1536	Dissolution of the Monasteries; Pilgrimage of Grace; union of England and Wales
1542	Battle of Solway Moss; English victory over invading Scottish army
1543	War with France
1547	Succession of Edward VI; ascendancy of Protector Somerset; battle of Pinkie: English victory over Scotland
1549	First Book of Common Prayer; Northumberland's coup
1553	Accession of Mary
1554	Pole returns; reunion with Rome; Wyatt's rebellion
1555	Persecution of Protestants begins
1557	War with France

1558	New Book of Rates; accession of Elizabeth I
1559	Peace of Cateau-Cambrésis; religious Settlement in England
1566	Archbishop Parker's *Advertisements* demand religious conformity
1568	Mary Stuart flees to England
1569	Northern Rebellion
1570	Papal bull declares Elizabeth excommunicated and deposed
1580	Jesuit missionaries arrive in England
1585	War with Spain
1587	Execution of Mary Stuart
1588	Defeat of the Spanish Armada
1594	Bad harvests begin
1601	Essex's rebellion
1603	Death of Elizabeth; accession of James VI of Scotland as James I; peace in Ireland; Millenary Petition of the Puritans
1604	Peace with Spain (treaty of London); Hampton Court Conference (king, bishops, Puritans)
1605	Gunpowder Plot, the last major Catholic conspiracy
1606–7	Failure of James's plans for union of kingdoms
1607	Settlement of Virginia
1609	Rebellion of the Northern Earls in Ireland; beginnings of the Planting of Ulster by Scots and English Protestants
1610	Failure of Great Contract (reform of royal finance)
1611	Publication of Authorized Version of the Bible (Anglican–Puritan co-operation)
1612	Death of Prince Henry, James's promising elder son
1613	Marriage of Princess Elizabeth to Elector Palatine, Protestant zealot, enmeshed Britain in continental politics
1617–29	Ascendancy of George Villiers, duke of Buckingham
1919–22	Inigo Jones designs the Banqueting House, the first major royal public building since the reign of Henry VIII
1620	Pilgrim Fathers inaugurate religious migration to New England

1622–3	Prince Charles and Buckingham go to Spain to woo the king's daughter and are rebuffed
1624–30	War with Spain
1625	Death of James I; accession of Charles I and marriage to Henrietta Maria, sister of Louis XIII of France
1626–9	War with France
1628	Petition of Right; publication of Harvey's work on the circulation of the blood; assassination of Buckingham
1629	Charles I dissolves Parliament, determines to govern without one
1630	Large-scale emigration to Massachusetts begins
1633	William Laud translated to be Archbishop of Canterbury
1634–40	Ship Money case
1637	Hampden's case supports Charles I's claim to collect Ship Money
1637–40	Breakdown of Charles's government of Scotland and two attempts to impose his will by force
1640	Long Parliament summoned
1641	Remodelling of government in England and Scotland; abolition of conciliar courts, abolition of prerogative taxation, triennial bill, Grand Remonstrance; rebellion of Ulster Catholics
1642	King's attempt on the Five Members; his withdrawal from London; the 19 Propositions; the resort of arms: Civil War
1643	King's armies prosper; Scots invade on side of Parliament
1644	Parliamentary armies prosper, especially in the decisive battle of the war, Marston Moor (June)
1645	'Clubmen' risings of armed neutrals threaten both sides; Royalist armies disintegrate, but parliamentary forces reorganized (New Model Army)
1646	King surrenders to the Scots; bishops and Book of Common Prayer abolished, Presbyterian Church established
1647	Army revolt; radical movements criticize parliamentary tyranny; king prevaricates

1648	Second Civil War: Scots now side with the king and are defeated; provincial risings (Kent, Colchester, South Wales, Yorks., etc.) crushed
1649	Trial and execution of Charles I: England a Republic
1649–53	Government by sovereign single-chamber assembly, the 'Rump' Parliament thoroughly purged of royalists and moderates
1649–50	Oliver Cromwell conquers Ireland (Drogheda massacre)
1650–2	Oliver Cromwell conquers Scotland (battles of Dunbar and Worcester)
1651	Thomas Hobbes's *Leviathan* published
1652–4	First Dutch War
1653	Cromwell dissolves Rump, creates the Nominated or Barebones Assembly; it surrenders power back to him, and he becomes Lord Protector under a paper constitution (*The Instrument of Government*)
1655–60	War with Spain
1655	Royalist insurrection (Penruddock's rising) is a complete failure
1657	*Instrument of Government* replaced by a parliamentary paper constitution, the *Humble Petition and Advice*; Cromwell rejects title of King and remains Lord Protector, but nominates his own House of Lords
1658	Cromwell dies and is succeeded by his son Richard
1659	Richard overthrown by the army; Rump restored but displeases many in the army
1660	Charles II restored
1662	Church of England restored; Royal Society receives its Charter
1663	Failure of first royal attempt to grant religious toleration
1665–7	Second Dutch War
1665	Great Plague (final major outbreak)
1666	Great Fire of London
1667	Milton's *Paradise Lost* published
1672–3	Failure of second royal attempt to grant religious toleration
1672–4	Third Dutch War

1674	Grain bounties introduced (England self-sufficient in food)
1678	Titus Oates and the Popish Plot; Bunyan's *Pilgrim's Progress*, part I, published
1679–81	The Exclusion Crisis; emergence of Whig and Tory parties
1683	The Rye House Plot; Whigs proscribed
1685	Charles II dies; accession of James II; rebellion by Charles II's protestant bastard, the duke of Monmouth, fails
1687	James II's Declaration of Indulgence; Tories proscribed; Newton's *Principia Mathematica* published
1688	James II's son born
1688	William of Orange invades: James II takes flight, accession of William III (of Orange) and Mary

VOL. 4 THE EIGHTEENTH CENTURY AND THE AGE OF INDUSTRY

1689	Bill of Rights settles succession to the throne and declares illegal various grievances; Toleration Act grants rights to Trinitarian Protestant dissenters
1690	Battle of the Boyne: William III defeats Irish and French army
1694	Bank of England founded; death of Queen Mary; Triennial Act sets the maximum duration of a parliament at three years
1695	Lapse of Licensing Act
1697	Peace treaty of Ryswick between allied powers of the League of Augsburg and France; Civil List Act votes funds for the maintenance of the royal household
1701	War of Spanish Succession begins; Act of Settlement settles the royal succession on the descendants of Sophia of Hanover
1702	Death of William III; accession of Anne
1704	Battle of Blenheim: British, Dutch, German and Austrian troops defeat French and Bavarian forces; British capture of Gibraltar from Spain
1707	Union of England and Scotland
1710	Impeachment of Dr Sacheverell; Harley ministry
1713	Peace treaty of Utrecht concludes the War of Spanish Succession

1714	Death of Anne; accession of George I
1715	Jacobite rebellion aimed at overthrowing the Hanoverian succession fails
1716	Septennial Act sets the maximum duration of a parliament at seven years
1717	Whig split; suspension of convocation
1720	South Sea Bubble: many investors ruined after speculation in the stock of the South Sea Company
1721	Walpole ministry
1722	Atterbury Plot, the most notable Jacobite plot
1726	Jonathan Swift's *Gulliver's Travels* published
1727	Death of George I; accession of George II
1729	Alexander Pope's *Dunciad* published
1730	Walpole/Townshend split
1733	Excise crisis: Walpole has to abandon his plans to reorganize the customs and excise
1737	Death of Queen Caroline
1738	Wesley's 'conversion': the start of Methodism
1739	War of Jenkins' Ear: Anglo-Spanish naval war
1740	War of the Austrian Succession
1741	Samuel Richardson's *Pamela* published
1742	Fall of Walpole
1744	Ministry of Pelham
1745	Jacobite Rebellion led by 'Bonnie Prince Charlie'
1746	Battle of Culloden: the duke of Cumberland routs the Jacobite army
1748	Peace of Aix-la-Chapelle concludes War of the Austrian Succession
1752	Adoption of Gregorian Calendar
1753	Jewish Naturalization Bill
1754	Newcastle ministry
1756	Seven Years War: Britain allied with Frederick the Great of Prussian against France, Austria, and Russia
1757	Pitt–Newcastle ministry; battle of Plassey: British victory over Bengal
1759	Capture of Quebec: British victory over the French
1760	Death of George II; accession of George III
1761	Laurence Sterne's *Tristram Shandy* published
1762	Bute's ministry
1763	Peace of Paris concludes Seven Years War; Grenville

	ministry; Wilkes and General Warrants
1765	Rockingham ministry; American Stamp Act attempts to make the defence of the American colonies self-financing: repealed 1766
1766	Chatham ministry
1768	Grafton ministry; Middlesex election crisis
1769	James Watt's steam engine patented
1770	Lord North's ministry; Edmund Burke's *Thoughts on the Present Discontents* published; Falkland Islands crisis
1773	Boston Tea Party: American colonists protest against the East India Company's monopoly of tea exports to America
1774	Coercive Acts passed in retaliation for Boston Tea Party
1776	Declaration of American Independence; Edward Gibbon's *Decline and Fall* and Adam Smith's *Wealth of Nations* published
1779	Wyvill's Association movement
1780	Gordon Riots develop from a procession to petition parliament against the Catholic Relief Act
1781	Surrender at Yorktown: American victory over British troops
1782	Second Rockingham ministry
1783	Shelburne ministry; Peace of Versailles recognizes independence of American colonies; Fox–North coalition; Younger Pitt's ministry
1784	East India Act
1785	Pitt's motion for parliamentary reform defeated
1786	Eden commercial treaty with France
1789	French Revolution
1790	Edmund Burke's *Reflections on the Revolution in France* published
1791	Thomas Paine's *The Rights of Man* published
1792	Coal gas used for lighting; Mary Wollstonecraft's *Vindication of the Rights of Women* published
1793	Outbreak of war with France; voluntary Board of Agriculture set up; commercial depression
1795	'Speenhamland' system of outdoor relief adopted, making up wages to equal cost of subsistence

1796	Vaccination against smallpox introduced
1798	T. R. Malthus's *Essay on Population* published; tax of ten per cent on incomes over £200 introduced
1799	Trade Unions suppressed; Napoleon appointed First Consul in France
1799–1801	Commercial boom
1801	Union with Ireland; first British Census
1802	Peace with France; Peel introduces first factory legislation
1803	War with France; General Enclosure Act simplifies process of enclosure of common land
1805	Battle of Trafalgar: Nelson defeats the French and Spanish fleets
1809–10	Commercial boom
1811	Depression because of Orders in Council; 'Luddite' disturbances in Nottinghamshire and Yorkshire; George, Prince of Wales, made Prince Regent
1813	East India Company's monopoly abolished
1815	Battle of Waterloo: defeat of Napoleon; peace in Europe: Congress of Vienna; Corn Law passed setting price of corn at 80s. per quarter
1815–17	Commercial boom
1817	Slump; the Blanketeers' march and other disturbances
1819	Peterloo massacre: troops intervene at mass reform meeting, killing 11 and wounding 400
1820	Death of George III; accession of George IV
1821–3	Famine in Ireland
1824	Commercial boom
1825	Trade Unions legalized; Stockton and Darlington railway opens; commercial depression
1829	Catholic Emancipation, ending most denials or restrictions of Catholic civil rights, ownership of property, and holding of public office
1830	Death of George IV; accession of William IV; Liverpool and Manchester railway opens
1830–2	First major cholera epidemic; Whigs in power under Grey
1831	'Swing' riots in rural areas against the mechanization of agriculture
1832	Great Reform Bill brings climax to period of political

reform, enlarging the franchise and restructuring
representation in Parliament

1833   Factory Act limits child labour; beginning of Oxford
       Movement in Anglican Church

1834   Slavery abolished in the British Empire; parish
       workhouses instituted; Robert Owen founds the
       Grand National Consolidated Trade Union: action
       by government against 'illegal oaths' in unionism
       results in failure of GNCTU and transportation of
       six 'Tolpuddle Martyrs'

1835   Municipal Reform Act extends local government
       franchise to all ratepayers

1835–6 Commercial boom: 'little' railway mania

1837   Death of William IV; accession of Queen Victoria

1838   Anti-Corn Law League established; People's Charter
       drafted

1839   Chartist riots

1840   Penny post instituted

1841   Tories in power: Peel ministry

1844   Bank Charter Act; Rochdale Co-operative Society
       founded; Royal Commission on Health of Towns

1844–5 Railway mania: massive speculation and investment
       leads to building of 5,000 miles of track; potato
       famine begins in Ireland

1846   Corn Law abolished; Whigs in power

1848   Revolutions in Europe; Public Health Act

VOL. 5 THE MODERN AGE

1851   Great Exhibition

1852   Derby's first minority Conservative government

1852–5 Aberdeen's coalition government

1853   Gladstone's first budget

1854   Northcote–Trevelyan civil service report

1854–6 Crimean War, defending European interests in the
       Middle East against Russia

1855   Palmerston's first government

1857–8 Second Opium War opens China to European trade

1858–9 Derby's second minority Conservative government

1858   Indian Mutiny and India Act

1859   Publication of Darwin's *Origin of Species*

1882	Britain occupies Egypt; Triple Alliance between Germany, Austria, and Italy
1884–5	Reform and Redistribution Acts
1885	Death of Gordon at Khartoum; Burma annexed; Salisbury's first (minority) Conservative government
1886	Royal Niger Company chartered; gold found in Transvaal; Gladstone's third Liberal government introduces first Home Rule Bill for Ireland: Liberal Party splits
1886–92	Salisbury's second (Conservative–Liberal-Unionist) government
1887	British East Africa Company chartered
1888	County Councils Act establishes representative county authorities
1889	London dock strike; British South Africa Company chartered
1892–4	Gladstone's fourth (minority) Liberal government
1893	Second Home Rule Bill rejected by the Lords; Independent Labour Party founded
1894–5	Rosebery's minority Liberal government
1895–1902	Salisbury's third Unionist ministry
1896–8	Sudan conquered
1898	German naval expansion begins
1899–1902	Second Anglo-Boer War
1899	(autumn)British disasters in South Africa
1900	Khaki election won by Salisbury; formation of Labour Representation Committee; Commonwealth of Australia Act
1901	Death of Victoria; accession of Edward VII
1902	Balfour's Education Act; Anglo-Japanese alliance
1902–5	Balfour's Unionist government
1903	Chamberlain's Tariff Reform campaign starts
1904	Anglo-French *Entente*
1905–8	Campbell-Bannerman's Liberal government
1906	Liberals win general election (January); Labour Party formed
1907	Anglo-Russian *Entente*
1908–15	Asquith's Liberal government
1908	Asquith's Old Age Pensions plan introduced

1909	Churchill's Employment Exchanges introduced; Lloyd George's budget rejected by Lords; Union of South Africa Act
1910	(January) General election: Liberal government retains office
	(May) Death of Edward VII; accession of George V
	(December) General election: Liberal government again retains office
1911	Parliament Act curtails power of the House of Lords, establishes five-yearly elections; Lloyd George's National Insurance Act; Moroccan crisis
1911–12	Railway, mining, and coal strikes
1912	Anglo-German navy talks fail
1912–14	Third Home Rule Act (for Ireland) and Welsh Church Disestablishment Act passed, but suspended
1914	(28 June) Assassination of Archduke Ferdinand at Sarajevo
	(4 August) British Empire enters the First World War
1915–16	Dardanelles expedition, ending in British withdrawal from Gallipoli
1916	Battle of the Somme; battle of Jutland; Lloyd George succeeds Asquith as Prime Minister
1917	Battle of Passchendaele
1918	End of First World War (11 November); Lloyd George coalition government returned in 'coupon election' (December)
1919	Treaty of Versailles establishes peace in Europe
1921	Miners seek support of dockers' and railwaymen's unions (the 'Triple Alliance') in major strike: on 'Black Friday' the dockers and railwaymen back down, and the alliance is broken; Lloyd George concludes treaty with Sinn Fein
1922	Fall of Lloyd George; Bonar Law heads Conservative government
1923	Baldwin becomes Conservative Prime Minister; general election
1924	(January) MacDonald leads first Labour government
	(November) Conservatives return to office under Baldwin

1925	Britain goes back on the gold standard
1926	General Strike (3–12 May)
1929	General election; MacDonald leads second Labour government
1931	Financial crisis and run on the pound; Britain abandons the gold standard; MacDonald resigns and is returned in the election to head National government
1932	Ottawa Conference on imperial trade institutes protective tarriffs
1935	Conservatives win general election: Baldwin succeeds MacDonald as Prime Minister; Hoare–Laval pact on Abyssinia; Government of India Act
1936	Death of King George V; abdication of Edward VIII: George VI becomes king
1937	Neville Chamberlain succeeds Baldwin as Conservative Prime Minister
1938	Chamberlain meets Hitler at Berchtesgaden, Godesberg, and Munich
1939	British guarantee to Poland; British Empire declares war on Germany (3 September)
1940	Churchill succeeds Chamberlain as Prime Minister; withdrawal from Dunkirk; Battle of Britain
1941	*Luftwaffe* 'blitz' on many British cities; Soviet Union and United States enter the war
1942	Loss of Singapore; Montgomery's victory at El Alamein; battle of Stalingrad; Beveridge Report on social security
1943	Successful campaign in North Africa; Anglo-American armies invade Italy
1944	D-day invasion of France; Butler's Education Act
1945	End of war in Europe (8 May) and in far East (15 August); general election: massive Labour victory and Attlee becomes Prime Minister
1947	Coal and other industries nationalized; convertibility crisis; transfer of power to independent India, Pakistan, and Burma
1949	NATO founded; devaluation of the pound by Cripps
1950	General election: Labour retains power by narrow

majority; outbreak of war in Korea

1951   Festival of Britain; general election: Conservatives
        defeat Labour, and Churchill again becomes Prime
        Minister

1952   Death of King George VI; Queen Elizabeth II
        proclaimed

1954   British troops withdraw from Egypt

1955   Eden becomes Prime Minister; general election won by
        Conservatives

1956   Anglo-French invasion of Suez, followed by withdrawal

1957   Eden resigns; Macmillan becomes Prime Minister

1959   General election: Conservatives win with larger
        majority

1963   French veto Britain's application to join the European
        Common Market; test-ban treaty in Moscow limits
        nuclear testing; Douglas-Home succeeds Macmillan
        as Prime Minister

1964   General election: Labour under Harold Wilson win
        narrow majority

1966   General election: Labour win with much larger
        majority

1967   Devaluation of the pound

1970   General election: Conservatives under Edward Heath
        returned to office

1972   National miners' strike; Stormont government abolished
        in Northern Ireland

1973   Britain enters European Common Market

1974   National miners' strike; two general elections: Labour
        under Harold Wilson win both with narrow
        majorities

1975   Popular referendum confirms British membership of
        the Common Market

1976   Economic crisis: Britain obtains help from
        International Monetary Fund

1979   Devolution referendums in Wales and Scotland;
        general election: Conservatives under Mrs Thatcher
        returned to office; independence granted to
        Zimbabwe (Rhodesia)

1980   Britain becomes self-sufficient in North Sea oil

1981	Social Democratic Party founded
1982	Britain defeats Argentina in war over the Falkland Islands
1983	General election: Mrs Thatcher's Conservative government returned with massive majority; Cruise missiles installed
1984	Miners' strike
1985	Miners' strike ends after a year; Anglo-Irish Hillsborough Agreement signed
1986	Channel Tunnel treaty signed; 'Big Bang' in Stock Exchange
1987	General election: Mrs Thatcher's Conservative government again returned with a majority of over 100; Stock Exchange collapse in the autumn
1989	Poll tax introduced
1990	Resignation of Mrs Thatcher; John Major becomes Prime Minister
1991	Gulf War against Iraq

THE TUDORS
1485–1603

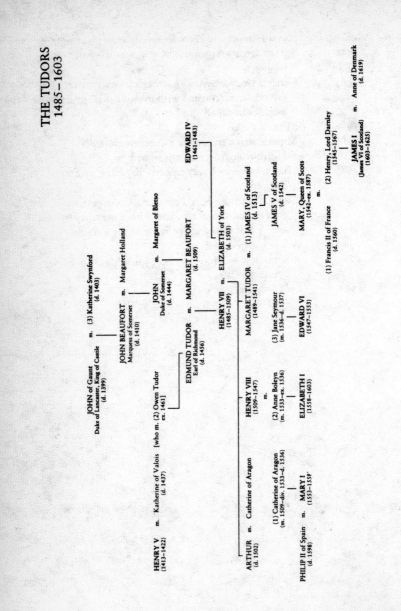

THE STUARTS
1603–1714

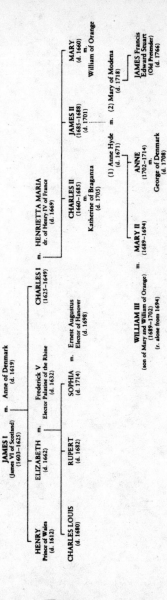

OXFORD

MORE OXFORD PAPERBACKS

This book is just one of nearly 1000 Oxford Paperbacks currently in print. If you would like details of other Oxford Paperbacks, including titles in the World's Classics, Oxford Reference, Oxford Books, OPUS, Past Masters, Oxford Authors, and Oxford Shakespeare series, please write to:

UK and Europe: Oxford Paperbacks Publicity Manager, Arts and Reference Publicity Department, Oxford University Press, Walton Street, Oxford OX2 6DP.

Customers in UK and Europe will find Oxford Paperbacks available in all good bookshops. But in case of difficulty please send orders to the Cash-with-Order Department, Oxford University Press Distribution Services, Saxon Way West, Corby, Northants NN18 9ES. Tel: 0536 741519; Fax: 0536 746337. Please send a cheque for the total cost of the books, plus £1.75 postage and packing for orders under £20; £2.75 for orders over £20. Customers outside the UK should add 10% of the cost of the books for postage and packing.

USA: Oxford Paperbacks Marketing Manager, Oxford University Press, Inc., 200 Madison Avenue, New York, N.Y. 10016.

Canada: Trade Department, Oxford University Press, 70 Wynford Drive, Don Mills, Ontario M3C 1J9.

Australia: Trade Marketing Manager, Oxford University Press, G.P.O. Box 2784Y, Melbourne 3001, Victoria.

South Africa: Oxford University Press, P.O. Box 1141, Cape Town 8000.

HISTORY IN OXFORD PAPERBACKS

Oxford Paperbacks offers a comprehensive list of books on British history, ranging from Frank Stenton's *Anglo-Saxon England* to John Guy's *Tudor England*, and from Christopher Hill's *A Turbulent, Seditious, and Factious People* to Kenneth O. Morgan's *Labour in Power: 1945–1951*.

TUDOR ENGLAND
John Guy

Tudor England is a compelling account of political and religious developments from the advent of the Tudors in the 1460s to the death of Elizabeth I in 1603.

Following Henry VII's capture of the Crown at Bosworth in 1485, Tudor England witnessed far-reaching changes in government and the Reformation of the Church under Henry VIII, Edward VI, Mary, and Elizabeth; that story is enriched here with character studies of the monarchs and politicians that bring to life their personalities as well as their policies.

Authoritative, clearly argued, and crisply written, this comprehensive book will be indispensable to anyone interested in the Tudor Age.

'lucid, scholarly, remarkably accomplished . . . an excellent overview' *Sunday Times*

'the first comprehensive history of Tudor England for more than thirty years' Patrick Collinson, *Observer*

Also in Oxford Paperbacks:

John Calvin   William J. Bouwsma
Early Modern France 1515–1715   Robin Briggs
The Spanish Armada   Felipe Fernández-Armesto
Time in History   G. J. Whitrow

HISTORY IN OXFORD PAPERBACKS

Oxford Paperbacks' superb history list offers books on a wide range of topics from ancient to modern times, whether general period studies or assessments of particular events, movements, or personalities.

THE STRUGGLE FOR
THE MASTERY OF EUROPE 1848–1918
A. J. P. Taylor

The fall of Metternich in the revolutions of 1848 heralded an era of unprecedented nationalism in Europe, culminating in the collapse of the Hapsburg, Romanov, and Hohenzollern dynasties at the end of the First World War. In the intervening seventy years the boundaries of Europe changed dramatically from those established at Vienna in 1815. Cavour championed the cause of *Risorgimento* in Italy; Bismarck's three wars brought about the unification of Germany; Serbia and Bulgaria gained their independence courtesy of the decline of Turkey—'the sick man of Europe'; while the great powers scrambled for places in the sun in Africa. However, with America's entry into the war and President Wilson's adherence to idealistic internationalist principles, Europe ceased to be the centre of the world, although its problems, still primarily revolving around nationalist aspirations, were to smash the Treaty of Versailles and plunge the world into war once more.

A. J. P. Taylor has drawn the material for his account of this turbulent period from the many volumes of diplomatic documents which have been published in the five major European languages. By using vivid language and forceful characterization, he has produced a book that is as much a work of literature as a contribution to scientific history.

'One of the glories of twentieth-century writing.' *Observer*

Also in Oxford Paperbacks:

Portrait of an Age: Victorian England   G. M. Young
Germany 1866–1945   Gorden A. Craig
The Russian Revolution 1917–1932   Sheila Fitzpatrick
France 1848–1945   Theodore Zeldin

OXFORD LIVES

Biography at its best—this acclaimed series offers authoritative accounts of the lives of men and women from the arts, sciences, politics, and many other walks of life.

STANLEY

Volume I: The Making of an African Explorer
Volume II: Sorceror's Apprentice
Frank McLynn

Sir Henry Morton Stanley was one of the most fascinating late-Victorian adventurers. His historic meeting with Livingstone at Ujiji in 1871 was the journalistic scoop of the century. Yet behind the public man lay the complex and deeply disturbed personality who is the subject of Frank McLynn's masterly study.

In his later years, Stanley's achievements exacted a high human cost, both for the man himself and for those who came into contact with him. His foundation of the Congo Free State on behalf of Leopold II of Belgium, and the Emin Pasha Relief Expedition were both dubious enterprises which tarnished his reputation. They also revealed the complex—and often troubling—relationship that Stanley has with Africa.

'excellent . . . entertaining, well researched and scrupulously annotated' *Spectator*

'another biography of Stanley will not only be unnecessary, but almost impossible, for years to come' *Sunday Telegraph*

Also available:

Carpet Sahib: A Life of Jim Corbett   Martin Booth
Bonnie Prince Charlie: Charles Edward Stuart   Frank McLynn

OXFORD LETTERS AND MEMOIRS

Letters, memoirs, and journals offer a special insight into the private lives of public figures and vividly recreate the times in which they lived. This popular series makes available the best and most entertaining of these documents, bringing the past to life in a fresh and personal way.

RICHARD HOGGART

A Local Habitation
Life and Times: 1918–1940

With characteristic candour and compassion, Richard Hoggart evokes the Leeds of his boyhood, where as an orphan, he grew up with his grandmother, two aunts, an uncle, and a cousin in a small terraced back-to-back.

'brilliant . . . a joy as well as an education' Roy Hattersley

'a model of scrupulous autobiography' Edward Blishen, *Listener*

A Sort of Clowning
Life and Times: 1940–1950

Opening with his wartime exploits in North Africa and Italy, this sequel to *A Local Habitation* recalls his teaching career in North-East England, and charts his rise in the literary world following the publication of *The Uses of Literacy*.

'one of the classic autobiographies of our time' Anthony Howard, *Independent on Sunday*

'Hoggart [is] the ideal autobiographer' Beryl Bainbridge, *New Statesman and Society*

Also in Oxford Letters and Memoirs:

My Sister and Myself: The Diaries of J. R. Ackerley
The Letters of T. E. Lawrence
A London Family 1870–1900   Molly Hughes

PAST MASTERS

General Editor: Keith Thomas

The *Past Masters* series offers students and general readers alike concise introductions to the lives and works of the world's greatest literary figures, composers, philosophers, religious leaders, scientists, and social and political thinkers.

'Put end to end, this series will constitute a noble encyclopaedia of the history of ideas.' Mary Warnock

HOBBES

Richard Tuck

Thomas Hobbes (1588–1679) was the first great English political philosopher, and his book *Leviathan* was one of the first truly modern works of philosophy. He has long had the reputation of being a pessimistic atheist, who saw human nature as inevitably evil, and who proposed a totalitarian state to subdue human failings. In this new study, Richard Tuck shows that while Hobbes may indeed have been an atheist, he was far from pessimistic about human nature, nor did he advocate totalitarianism. By locating him against the context of his age, Dr Tuck reveals Hobbs to have been passionately concerned with the refutation of scepticism in both science and ethics, and to have developed a theory of knowledge which rivalled that of Descartes in its importance for the formation of modern philosophy.

Also available in Past Masters:

Spinoza   Roger Scruton
Bach   Denis Arnold
Machiavelli   Quentin Skinner
Darwin   Jonathan Howard

PAST MASTERS

General Editor: Keith Thomas

The people whose ideas have made history . . .

'One begins to wonder whether any intelligent person can afford not to possess the whole series.' *Expository Times*

JESUS

Humphrey Carpenter

Jesus wrote no books, but the influence of his life and teaching has been immeasurable. Humphrey Carpenter's account of Jesus is written from the standpoint of an historian coming fresh to the subject without religious preconceptions. And no previous knowledge of Jesus or the Bible on the reader's part is assumed.

How reliable are the Christian 'Gospels' as an account of what Jesus did or said? How different were his ideas from those of his contemporaries? What did Jesus think of himself? Humphrey Carpenter begins his answer to these questions with a survey and evaluation of the evidence on which our knowledge of Jesus is based. He then examines his teaching in some detail, and reveals the perhaps unexpected way in which his message can be said to be original. In conclusion he asks to what extent Jesus's teaching has been followed by the Christian Churches that have claimed to represent him since his death.

'Carpenter's *Jesus* is about as objective as possible, while giving every justifiable emphasis to the real and persistent forcefulness of the moral teaching of this charismatic personality.' Kathleen Nott, *The Times*

'an excellent, straightforward presentation of up-to-date scholarship' David L. Edwards, *Church Times*

Also available in Past Masters:

Muhammad   Michael Cook
Aquinas   Anthony Kenny
Cervantes   P. E. Russell
Clausewitz   Michael Howard